THE HUT HANDBOOK

A Guide to Planning and Enjoying a Backcountry Hut Trip

Written and compiled by
Leigh Girvin Yule and Scott Toepfer

Illustrations by
Mara Mactaggart

WESTCLIFFE PUBLISHERS

Englewood, Colo

International Standard Book Number 1-56579-193-2
©1996 Leigh Girvin Yule and Scott Toepfer

Library of Congress Cataloging-in-Publication Data

Yule, Leigh Girvin.
    The hut handbook : a guide to planning and enjoying a backcountry hut
trip / written and compiled by Leigh Girvin Yule and Scott Toepfer ; illustrations by
Mara Mactaggart.
        p.   cm.
    Includes bibliographical references and index.
    ISBN 1-56579-193-2
    1. Snow camping—Handbooks, manuals, etc.   2. Mountaineering—Handbooks,
manuals, etc.   3. Backpacking—Handbooks, manuals, etc.   4. Huts.   I. Toepfer, Scott.
II. Title.
GV198.9.Y85   1996
796.5'22—dc20   96-44812
                                                                          CIP

Publisher: John Fielder
Production Manager: Harlene Finn
Designer: Mark Mulvany
Editors: Knox Williams, Elisa Adler
Cover photos by Brian Litz, *top:* Jackal Hut, 10th Mountain Division Hut Association,
Colorado, *bottom:* Utah's canyon country on the San Juan Hut System.

Permission to use quote by Bob Shacochis, page 100, granted from *Outside Magazine* © July
1996. Permission to use the quote, by David McClung and Peter Schaerer, page 55, from *The
Avalanche Book* granted from the Mountaineers Publishers.

Published by Westcliffe Publishers, Inc.
2650 South Zuni Street
Englewood, Colorado 80110
Phone (303) 935-0900 Fax (303) 935-0903

Printed in the United States of America

PLEASE NOTE: Risk is always a factor in backcountry and high-mountain travel. Many of the
activities described in this book can be dangerous, especially when weather is adverse or
unpredictable, and whenever unforseen events or conditions create a hazardous situation.
The authors have done their best to provide the reader with accurate information about
backcountry travel, as well as to point out some of its potential hazards. It is the responsibility of the users of this guide to learn the necessary skills for safe ski touring and backcountry travel, and to exercise caution in potentially hazardous areas, especially on glaciers and
in avalanche-prone terrain. The authors and publisher disclaim any liability for injury or
other damage done by anyone ski touring, snowshoeing, mountain biking, hiking, snow-
boarding, telemark skiing, sledding, horseback riding, using the huts, or any other activity
described in this book.

*For more information about other fine books and calendars from Westcliffe Publishers, please
contact your local bookstore or write, call, or fax for our free color catalogue.*

CONTENTS

ACKNOWLEDGMENTS

When we first decided to write this book we thought we'd be able to do it with a little help from our friends. How mistaken we were! The existence of this book not only depended on the unwavering support of our friends but also on the generous help from our neighbors, bosses, families, various government agencies, and even people we had never met who came to our aid during the long hours we spent writing and compiling information.

Much help came from active members of the Summit Huts Association (SHA) who contributed to, read, and critiqued *The Hut Handbook*. We are especially grateful to John Warner, D.D.S., John Cooley, Chris Pizzo, M.D., and Pete Wingle for their contributions to the content of this book, as well as to Cindy Gray, Tim and Patti Casey, Thane Wright, Mike Zobbe and Greg Walter for keeping SHA on the right track.

Paul Parker's understanding of the subtleties of contracts and working with contributors was as indispensable as his section on the telemark turn.

Brian Litz was extremely generous in helping to put this guide together and in sharing his knowledge of publishing, photographs, and the hut experience.

A big thanks to Dale Atkins for his section on rescue.

The United States Forest Service was helpful in providing us with information on various hut systems throughout the western United States. The Colorado Division of Wildlife helped with data on wildlife. Special thanks to Paul Semmer of the White River National Forest for his assistance.

Scott's wintertime boss, Knox Williams, donated much appreciated time and helped to get the book to press.

Other readers who gave us their input and who deserve thanks are Ellen Hollinshead and Judy Girvin.

Many folks with the 10th Mountain Division Huts Association (TMDHA) contributed historical facts and humorous anecdotes to the book. Thanks to Peter Looram, David Schweppe, Scott Messina, Jarod Trow, Karen Bellina, Erica Hall, and Cindy Carpenter. Thank you also to two 10th Mountain board members, Robert McNamara and Ben Eiseman, M.D.

A huge thank-you goes to Mara Mactaggart for her wonderful illustrations that she completed in such a short period of time.

A special thanks to Scott's mother who wants to buy the first 300 copies of the book for all the relatives and to Leigh's husband for his patience and delicious Mexican dinners.

Finally, we owe our special gratitude to John Fielder for donating time from his hectic schedule to help get this book published within a budget that keeps it affordable, and to Harlene Finn, Linda Doyle, and Amy Duenkel for marshalling it through the process.

A portion of the proceeds from the sale of this book benefit Summit Huts Association, a not-for-profit organization dedicated to developing and managing a system of back-country cabins lined by non-motorized trails in Summit County, Colorado.

INTRODUCTION

Imagine the welcome sight of a rustic, backcountry cabin after traveling on your own power through wild and majestic mountains. The cabin is stocked with firewood, pots and pans, beds and pillows. No telephone will be ringing when you get there, no running water dripping in the sink. No on-site manager will interrupt you. Solar power, lanterns, or candles are your only sources of light once the sun goes down. You supply your own food and fall into the sleeping bag you have carried with you. You fix your own meals, keep the cabin clean, and haul out your trash. It takes a lot of work, but you know it's worth it—the peace and serenity of a backcountry experience are yours to enjoy.

The hut experience described in this book requires "self-catering." While some hut systems, such as the renowned Appalachian Mountain Club cabins and Europe's Haute Route, provide food, bedding, and staff to clean, cook, and wash your dishes, in this book we focus on the self-sufficient backcountry hut adventure. Even though much of the information carries over from season to season, we emphasize winter, since winter is the most popular season for hut use.

Hut users must be conscientious and educated not only in backcountry ethics but also in the proper use of the huts. This will ensure the continued success of the hut system. The purpose of this book is to provide the reader, whether novice heading out for the first time or seasoned hut veteran, with helpful information.

In *The Hut Handbook* we describe the huts and yurts and your responsibilities when using them. We give you planning guidelines, equipment lists, troubleshooting hints, and suggest what to do if you don't make it to the hut. We include basic information on first aid, route-finding, map reading, and natural hazards. This information is only basic, however; there isn't enough space in *The Hut Handbook* to include an in-depth discussion on everything you need to know about first aid, route-finding, maps, or hazards. We urge you to read additional books on these subjects and to take some of the many important courses now available to further your backcountry knowledge before you head out.

We do not describe specific routes here, or give directions on how to reach any of the huts. Detailed trail descriptions are covered in several guidebooks to Colorado, Appalachian Mountain, and Canadian huts. Please see our bibliography for information on these excellent resources.

Hut systems are maintained throughout the mountains of North America, and this book will be applicable to all of them. *The Hut Handbook* emphasizes Colorado only because Colorado is our base of operations and also the state with the largest and most extensive hut systems.

A hut adventure is a vacation, camping trip, and wilderness trek. *The Hut Handbook* gives you the information and tips that we hope will help make your adventure safe, enjoyable, and memorable for years to come.

WHY "DO A HUT TRIP?"

Afoot and light-hearted I take to the open road,
Healthy, free, the world before me,
The long brown path before me, leading wherever I choose.
—*Walt Whitman (1819-1892)*

Why "do a hut trip?" Why would we strap a heavy pack onto our backs, trudge for miles through the woods, and climb high mountains, just to spend the night in some remote cabin without electricity, running water, or plumbing facilities, and with people we don't even know?

The answer lies in the fact that we're after adventure. That's what a hut trip promises us. It takes us outside and beyond our ordinary lives. We rise to the challenge of whatever the natural elements deal us.

Adventure is fun and that is its greatest appeal. But fun means different things to different people. For the person who enjoys the outdoors, a hut trip combines the best of the outdoor experience: spending time on the trail traveling to a destination, carrying only those items we need for our basic survival in the woods, using all our backcountry skills, yet arriving at a comfortable shelter instead of a dripping snow cave or a cold tent. On the way we meet new people who share similar interests.

Even more than the fun it provides, a hut trip allows us to feel that we are part of something larger than ourselves. We sense a connection to the community of people who know and love the hut experience and who labor to make it work. The huts are there for all of us who adhere to the self-sufficient backcountry ethic, one that calls for traveling and living lightly on the land.

Once you reach the hut, you'll probably feel like you've been gone a long time, even if you're out for just one night. In a hut, you literally and figuratively "get away from it all."

McNamara Hut, 10th Mountain Division Hut Association System near Aspen, Colorado. Photo by Brian Litz

There's time with family and friends without the distractions of work, television, telephone, or traffic. And a hut adventure gives you shared memories to talk about for the rest of your life. "Remember the time it snowed so hard we couldn't find the trail?" "Remember when we got so scared from Jeffrey's ghost stories that the three of us had to go to the outhouse together!" "Wasn't it hilarious watching Ted learn to telemark ski!"

A hut trip helps people understand and appreciate the natural world. Guests see the fragile balance in which plants and animals live and support each other. They experience how solar energy can be captured for light and heat, how every drop of water must be used wisely because it is precious. The circumspect hut user may see huts as a metaphor for how we need to live and conserve the earth's resources.

These trips are not without risk, which is partly why they can be such a grand adventure. They offer a rare opportunity for us to challenge ouselves, weigh the risks involved, and make critical decisions. In the backcountry, no highway patrol pulls up to help with a broken binding. No ambulance arrives to care for a sprained wrist or broken ankle. There are few trail signs to give directions, and sometimes there's no visible trail. You're on your own with your wits, your skills, and your friends.

QUOTABLES

It's like Ponce de Leon looking for the fountain of youth. Every year I go out with a group for three or four days. Many of us will be over 70 or 75 years old. We still have as much fun as we ever did.
   —Ben Eiseman, M.D.

I love the fantastic silence; you can almost feel the stillness. The grandeur and beauty of the mountains. . . the exhilaration of skiing up is incredible, but even better is skiing back down in waist-deep powder.
   —Robert McNamara

I think of the huts as a way to get back to the simplicity that skiing was all about. It was so simple, so easy, and inexpensive. It's a great family sport.
   —Fritz Benedict

COMMUNAL LIVING

The huts offer a unique experience in communal living. It requires the best from us—cooperation, communication, tolerance, sharing, and respect. For a successful hut experience the group must respect the individual, and the individual must also respect the group.

Guests share cooking and living and sleeping space. You might find yourself on a bunk above a stranger and trying to ignore someone else's irritating game of charades. It helps to know in advance that there's no privacy in a hut, and to plan and set your expectations accordingly.

But communal living can be fun and can make for wonderful anecdotes and memorable stories. You'll never forget when the other group ate all your food by mistake, and left your group with nothing but pancake mix for three more days. Nor will you ever forget that wizened old man who helped you fix the broken strap on your backpack before you set off on that cold and brilliant January morning.

The huts are governed by an honor system, and this fact continues to amaze newcomers to the hut experience. It is almost unfathomable in today's society that it is possible to be entrusted with the combination to a hut's lock with little more than the exchange of a credit card number. We feel good that we are trusted to care for the hut and for the land. Our esteem is boosted by the fact that others have faith in us to use the system properly. That good hut karma carries over to all other aspects of the hut experience.

Evening around the fire. Photo by Brian Litz

Wide-open spaces and spectacular vistas await the hut user. Photo by Scott Toepfer

Telemark skiing near St. Paul Lodge, Silverton, Colorado. Photo by Scott Toepfer

THE BACKCOUNTRY EXPERIENCE

Backcountry travel requires self-sufficiency. Trails may not be marked or packed. Good map and compass skills are essential for a successful hut trip.

Many people seek a backcountry hut experience in order to get away from it all, and they don't appreciate the noise or the smell of snowmobiles in the otherwise pristine winter environment. Motorized access to the huts is prohibited in some hut networks but may be permitted in others. In Colorado many huts are regulated by the U.S. Forest Service which protects huts inside a non-motorized "envelope" ranging from six to sixty acres. Forest Service regulation of snowmobiles in the backcountry helps to maintain an island of calm around the huts.

Paul Semmer, a community planner with the White River National Forest in Colorado, explained to us how the national forests are managed for multiple use and that we must "understand that the 'backyard' is not getting any bigger." Different kinds of people want to use the backcountry for different kinds of recreation, and the U.S. Forest Service attempts to accommodate all kinds of uses. For those of us who can't tolerate the possibility of seeing (or hearing) a snowmobile, winter camping in a designated wilderness area might be more enjoyable than travel to a hut where motorized access is allowed. Check for motorized regulations before planning your backcountry hut trip.

From the Logbook

Quiet, snow muffled world outside. No traffic. No barking dogs. No sirens. No car alarms. No phones, faxes, or televisions. Just quiet.

The adventure and challenge of being out in nasty weather, dealing with problems, solving them, and finally finding the route to the hut makes arriving to that warm shelter even more precious and wonderful.

Live by the sun and the hunger in your stomach. Go to bed only after Orion has risen. Rise at first light. Eat when you're hungry. Clocks don't matter.

Carry everything you need on your back. Live with the land. Solar energy, simple toilets, creeks or snowmelt for water. The huts teach you what you can do without. You wish you could live like this forever.

Everyone comes to a hut for a different reason. Some come to have a cardiovascular stress test without the formal monitoring. Others come to test the range of their cellular phones. Others are here to change the pattern of their daily life and reflect on why they remain in those patterns.

This final day has brought much gratitude and more appreciation for these beautiful lands above 11,000 feet. Life in the present. Traveling at the speed of happiness. Namaste.

Environmental Impacts of the Huts

The impacts of the huts on the environment are minimal in the winter when they receive their greatest use and when the land is protected by a layer of snow. Surrounding vegetation is insulated and protected. Trails disappear with the spring thaw, and many animals are safe in their winter dens or have gone to lower elevations until spring.

Many people argue, however, about whether or not summer hut use has a positive or negative impact on the surrounding environment. Those people who oppose summer use claim that the huts cause a substantial impact on the surrounding environment as they concentrate human activity into a small area. Opponents also cite the destruction of fragile vegetation, creation of new trails or erosion of old ones, smoke from wood fires, and the smell of humans which may frighten wild animals.

Summer use has proved to be beneficial in some areas, however. It was permitted at the Colorado's 10th Mountain Division Hut Association (TMDHA) cabins in the early 1990s, after many seasons of winter use only. Summer use at the huts has actually been shown to improve the environment in the surrounding areas because 10th Mountain revegetates disturbed areas, picks up trash, establishes trails, and provides staffing and management. Where once campers made dozens of fire rings, bathed in streams, and relieved themselves behind any bush or tree, the huts now consolidate human use to one area, thus helping to protect the backcountry.

A reflective moment. Photo by Brian Litz

ARGUMENTS AGAINST HUTS

Many people argue against the construction of new huts and the expansion of hut systems. Backcountry skiers don't want to see huts near their favorite powder stashes. Snowmobilers fear that more huts will lead to an increase in regulations against motorized vehicles. Wildlife advocates don't want to introduce more people into already fragmented habitats. Wilderness advocates don't want huts near wilderness areas because of the temptation of snowmobilers or mountain bikers to cross the wilderness boundary. Environmentalists don't want any more development in the backcountry. Nearby landowners don't want huts in the National

Forest above their homes because they will increase traffic on roads and at trailheads. Indeed, hut opponents are becoming increasingly strident in their efforts.

Dottie Fox, chair of the Aspen Wilderness Workshop and recent Wilderness Society honoree, says, "I love the huts. . .but the backcountry is a fragile ecosystem. . .and when people have easy access [to it] it leads to abuse of the backcountry."

Elizabeth Boyles, founding member and original staffer of TMDHA, disagrees. In a 10th Mountain Division newsletter she explained why she thinks the huts actually help to preserve the backcountry: "Though a far cry from an igloo, [huts] are just as far from the complicated lifestyles we lead in our modern world. The sun-powered lights, water collection, wood heat, the act of skiing to the huts; all these promote a sense of self-sufficiency that stays with us when we return to modern life. These simple dwellings can teach us to get by with less of the world's resources—and have fun in the process. People who love and travel the wilderness will help to protect it. The huts can only help with this."

WHAT'S NEXT FOR THE HUTS?

In the future huts will need to do more to justify their existence by providing educational programs, access for the disabled, and opportunities for research. Hut proponents will need to show extensive documentation on the need for more cabins and will be required to do more to mitigate the environmental and social impacts of huts in the backcountry.

Whether hut use has reached its peak remains to be seen. Directors of TMDHA expect to see hut use stabilize in the future, instead of continuing to increase dramatically. In recent years visits to the two huts of the 10th Mountain Division increased from 2,252 in 1984 to 17,813 visits at 10 huts in 1994. Economists who believe there aren't enough backcountry skiers and other outdoor enthusiasts to support a growing hut system help to confirm 10th Mountain's suspicion. Yet others believe that more huts mean more opportunities for more people to enjoy them. These people claim we must continue to build more huts in the backcountry.

Regardless of how many we have, the huts are built to last generations and will be with us for years to come. It is our responsibility to care for them. Only then can we be sure they'll be here in the future for our children and grandchildren to enjoy.

My First Hut Trip

It was with mild trepidation that the four of us women assembled at the Spruce Creek trailhead to make the 1,000- foot, 2.2-mile ascent to Francie's Cabin as part of the second annual Women's Hut Trip in mid-January 1996. The nervousness stemmed not only from our inexperience on cross-country skis and snow-shoes, but also from uncertainty over which trail to pursue and the cloudy, snow-threatening weather. Two hours later, our slow but steady pace yielded the log cabin at the crest of a steep slope.

While some of us rested in the chilly upstairs bedrooms, others chatted, read and played games as the afternoon sun dipped beyond the horizon. Our amiable chattering grew louder as wine bottles were uncorked and we relaxed in the camaraderie developed in exchanging adventure stories among the women.

Following a breakfast of half-cooked pancakes and fruit, we embarked on a morning ski trip to Crystal Lake, despite warnings of high avalanche danger. It was a quintessential Colorado scene — brilliant blue sky and staggering mountain peaks amid pillows of white fluffy snow. Our subsequent descent to the trailhead was less arduous and took only half the time of the climb. We nevertheless felt a sense of accomplishment and congratulated ourselves on a successful hut trip.

— Kay Christensen Goldsmith, Littleton, Colorado

2

HISTORY OF THE HUTS

. . . where the storm drives me
I turn in for shelter.
—Quintus Horatius
Flaccus (65-8 B.C.)

The first huts were simple shelters from the storm, places to get out of the weather. They evolved in Europe over the past two centuries from army barracks, customs stations, alpine hotels, and club refuges. The year 1888 marked the first hut built in the United States by the Appalachian Mountain Club which envisioned the hut as a backcountry refuge for hikers. Recent hut systems like Colorado's Alfred A. Braun Memorial Hut System, the 10th Mountain Division Huts, and Summit Huts were all modeled after the earlier European and Appalachian models.

EUROPEAN HUTS

The hut system, which still thrives in Europe today, was born in Scandinavia—not surprising since Nordic skiing started there. In Norway, where a hut system was founded in 1868, over 300 huts are connected by 18,000 km of trails. The huts vary from spartan shelters to "hut-els," complete with private rooms, showers, sauna, dining room, bar and lounge.

In central Europe, alpine clubs began building shelters for mountain climbers in the latter part of the nineteenth century. These shelters evolved into two well known hut systems, the Bernese Oberland in Switzerland, and the Haute Route, famous for its spectacular scenery and high traverse crossing the Alps from Chamonix, France to Zermatt, Switzerland with a brief step into Italy.

Some European huts are large, accomondating up to 150 people and offer food services and bedding. Some are lavish, others are spartan. Sleeping arrangements may vary from country to country: Austrian huts offer each guest an individual platform or bunk, while Swiss sleeping accommodations are more cozy—often shoulder to shoulder, causing one visitor to exclaim, "I don't sleep this close to my wife!"

TIPS FROM THE PROS

Euro hut-tripping is "soft mountaineering." "Soft" because you always have a warm hut, hot meal, and bed to crawl into after a day of rigorous activity, and staff to take care of you. It's "mountaineering" because you get to climb and ski spectacular peaks, passes, and glaciers, with all the attendant skills of rope handling, use of crampons, ice axes, and crevasse rescue lurking in the background.
— John Warner, D.D.S.

Hut near St. Moritz, Switzerland. Photo by John Warner

Canadian huts were first developed in the 1990s for day tour shelters. They weren't wolverine-proofed until the 1980s. Photo by Brian Litz

THE FIRST U.S. HUTS

Appalachian Mountain Club Huts

The first complete hut system in the United States was established by the Appalachian Mountain Club (AMC) in the White Mountains of New Hampshire. Madison Spring Hut was the first hut built along what later became the Appalachian Trail. A stone structure built in 1888, Madison Hut hosted its first overnight guests in February, 1889. The hut served AMC's goals of providing a base for scientific exploration and sheltering "trampers" who braved the elements of the Presidential Range. It must also have appealed to the AMC club members' sense of fun.

The vision of a network of AMC huts belongs to Joe Dodge who improved four simple huts along a 56 mile section of the Appalachian Trail and connected them with a system of cabins a day's hike apart. During his tenure as hutmaster from the 1920's to 1950's, Dodge built several more cabins along the Appalachian Trail.

Today, AMC offers a full-service summer hut experience, with food service, bedding, and staff to cook, wash dishes and clean the huts. Two huts are open in winter for self-service trampers.

Lakes Hut, looking down from Mount Monroe in New Hampshire. Photo by David Hoy/Appalachian Mountain Club

Tagert Hut of Colorado

The first hut in Colorado was Tagert Hut, named after Billy Tagert, a dam keeper for a mining operation who developed a passion for skiing late in his life. He lived in an old miner's cabin on the flanks of a mountain above Ashcroft near Aspen. In 1946, two backcountry enthusiasts from Aspen, Fritz Benedict and Stuart Mace, visited Tagert and persuaded him to let them equip the cabin for backcountry travels. They hid canned foods under the floorboards to be used during their frequent ski tours of the area.

Years later, the same Benedict established the 10th Mountain Division Hut Association. Mace, who managed the Tagert Hut for many years by soliciting one dollar donations from guests, also established the Toklat Chalet in Ashcroft. Soon other huts cropped up in the area to form a loose collection of cabins which eventually became the Alfred Braun Hut System. When the Tagert Hut burned to the ground in the 1950's, however, the budding hut system fell into limbo for many years.

Markley Hut, Alfred Braun Hut System, Colorado. Photo by Brian Litz

The Alfred A. Braun Memorial Hut System

Not until the 1960's was interest and activity in the huts renewed with the leadership of Fred Braun who oversaw the construction of five more cabins. A German by birth, Braun was a ski trooper in the Czech army. After his retirement in 1951 he moved to Aspen and founded Aspen Mountain Rescue, organized a chapter of the Colorado Mountain Club, and started the first ambulance service in town. The old network of rustic, remote mountain cabins was eventually renamed the Alfred Braun Memorial Hut System in recognition of his many contributions to the Aspen backcountry.

The 10th Mountain Division Hut Association

The 10th Mountain Division Hut Association was born from the friendship and common love of backcountry skiing of three men: Ben Eiseman, Fritz Benedict, and Robert McNamara, a seasoned climber and cross-country skier from Denver, Ben Eiseman had traveled Europe's Haute Route and knew the idea of a hut system would translate well to Colorado. He discovered an accessible backcountry ski route between Vail and Aspen, but it had a drawback—the avalanche prone areas in the Frying Pan Valley. At about the same time, Fritz Benedict was working on his own idea for a hut route in the same general area, one which avoided the hazards in Frying Pan Valley.

These two men might never have come together to create a hut route had it not been for the unfortunate death in 1981 of Ben Eiseman's friend, Margaret McNamara, wife of Robert McNamara, Secretary of Defense under President John F. Kennedy. McNamara wanted to memorialize his wife and to commemorate their love of skiing. Eiseman suggested that McNamara speak with Fred Braun about establishing a "Margy's Hut." Braun liked the idea and suggested erecting a prefabricated hut near Aspen. Benedict, an architect as well as a skier, offered to design the hut himself. Thus, the partnership was cemented.

It wasn't easy to convince the U.S. Forest Service to let them build a hut in the backcountry. "We had a heckuva lot of trouble with the Forest Service," McNamara remembers. "They had fifteen different reasons why we couldn't build a hut. One of their reasons was that huts wouldn't be used! I said, 'Give me time to promote them. If after five years huts aren't used as much as you feel they should be, I'll pay to have them removed.'"

Three years after Margy's Hut was built, McNamara tried to take his friend former U.S. Attorney General Elliott Richardson there. He tried to book three beds, three months in advance, but couldn't get a reservation. Needless to say, he didn't have to pay to have the huts removed.

In addition to Margy's Hut, built in 1982, the men built McNamara Hut, and a minihut system east of Aspen was soon established. Both huts were built, stocked with firewood, and outfitted by volunteers in a sixteen week period. Originally permitted by the U.S. Forest Service under the auspices of the United States Ski Association, Margy's and McNamara's Huts were later transferred to the 10th Mountain Division Hut Association upon that organization's founding in the mid-1980s.

To Benedict, the huts were a way to bring people closer to nature: "As life gets more and more complex and most people live in cities. . .connecting with nature is so important," he said in 1994, a year before his death.

Benedict was one of those rare people who could be called an environmentalist and a developer at the same time. An architect, planning commissioner, and visionary, he is credited with designing the community of Aspen, Colorado, with its pedestrian-friendly mall, trail systems, parks, and open space. He was also a World War II veteran, and member of the U.S. Army's 10th Mountain Division, a select group of young men who trained at Camp Hale in the backcountry between Leadville and Vail in Colorado. They learned mountain warfare, skiing, and winter survival skills there.

The 10th Mountain Division soldiers were the last division to be sent to Europe in World War II and played a pivotal role in a critical Italian battle. The mountain troopers took Riva Ridge from the Germans by scaling a sheer rock wall one cold winter night and surprising the enemy at daybreak. The capture of Riva Ridge allowed allied forces to drive the Germans out of Italy and eventually led to German surrender.

After the war many of the 10th Mountain Division soldiers returned to the mountains where they had their military training. Some of the men became leaders in the new Colorado ski industry. Says one 10th Mountain veteran, "[the huts] perpetuate the memory of the 10th Mountain Division . . .and our common love of the mountains."

Tenth Montain Division Hut Assosiation grew to ten huts in ten years. Today it surrounds the Holy Cross Wilderness and connects the communities of Vail, Leadville, and Aspen. It ties in with Crested Butte to the west via the Alfred Braun System and Summit County to the east via the Summit Huts Association system.

The huts capture Fritz Benedict's strong sense of community, creating "community" in the truest sense of the word—a group of people living under a common roof with common interests and goals.

Looking back to the early 1960s, I recall most fondly the backcountry ski trips down virtually every side of Mount Hood, Oregon. Backcountry skis did not exist. Low-cut boots, wood skis with pine tar bases, and bamboo poles were not good enough for alpine touring. We would ski the glaciers, climb to the peaks, and ridges with shouldered skis, and ski home. Fortunately, times have changed.
—*Pete Wingle*

Author Scott Toepfer relaxes at Margy's Hut, near Aspen, Colorado. Photo by Steve Huyler

3

CHOOSING YOUR HUT

Two roads diverged in a wood, and I—
I took the one less traveled by,
And that has made all the difference.
—*Robert Frost (1874-1963)*

Choosing your hut and the group with whom you'll share it are two of the most important decisions you'll make in planning your trip. You'll need to consider the skill level and compatibility of your group, the difficulty of the journey, and the equipment and food you'll need to bring. In this chapter we discuss considerations that go into deciding which hut is best for you.

CHOOSING THE GROUP

Choose your group first. Then select the hut best suited to your group's interests and abilities. When composing your group, look for compatibility among the group members, their skills, level of ability, how much weight they can carry, how well and how fast they can travel, whether children are included, and how many nights you'll be out together. Consider each person's potential strengths and weaknesses and how well they will be able to work as a team.

Time with friends. Photo by Todd Powell

GROUP ROLES

For a successful trip, each member of the group should have a clear understanding of his or her roles and responsibilities. Spread the work so that several people help organize and plan the outing. To help plan, we offer the following to-do checklist for seven roles to be assigned among the group members:

Trip Organizer:
___ Plan the trip
___ Choose the group
___ Make reservations
___ Study the confirmation information well in advance of the trip
___ Disseminate information such as liability waivers, equipment lists, cabin amenities, etc. to others in the group
___ Collect signed waivers and return to hut system manager
___ Handle any cancellations and changes
___ Participate in meal planning
___ Distribute food assignments
___ Plan and coordinate logistics such as travel to the trailhead or carpooling

___ Act as clearinghouse for logistics, meals, etc.
___ Carry confirmation letter and cabin combination or key
___ Make sure others have combination to cabin

Group Leader:
___ Oversee the group; responsible for route-finding, maps, and decision-making in the field
___ Perform equipment check before trip
___ Conduct group meeting prior to trip
___ Coordinate with first aid and avalanche experts (or possess these skills)
___ Carry a tool kit and binding repair kit

Hut Master/Mistress:
___ Familiarize yourself with the hut, its systems and operations upon arrival
___ Keep the fire burning
___ Oversee supplies of kindling and firewood
___ Direct operation of melting snow for water
___ Close up cabin on departure; lock windows and doors (See Chapter 16, Leaving the Hut)

Kitchen Master/Mistress:
___ Plan meals
___ Work with Trip Organizer on food assignments
___ Prepare food for trip or delegate preparation to others
___ Oversee meal preparation and dishwashing
___ Carry the kitchen kit (see Chapter 12, In the Kitchen)
___ Keep track of purified water
___ Organize and distribute trash for removal and recycling
___ Make sure kitchen is clean and organized

First Aid Expert:
___ Be proficient in emergency medical procedures, evacuation, wilderness rescue

Avalanche Expert:
___ Be proficient in determining avalanche hazard and avoidance
___ Consult with Group Leader in route-finding
___ Make sure everyone has proper gear
___ Conduct avalanche transceiver tests

Workers:
___ Gather snow, chop kindling, carry wood, prepare meals, wash dishes

THE SIZE OF THE GROUP

Just because there are seven or more roles for a successful hut trip doesn't mean you have to have seven people in your group. One person may act as a guide by taking on all of the group roles, or individuals can take on more than one role.

A group of two will travel more quickly and efficiently than a larger group. It's also easier to get reservations for two people than it is for larger parties, especially during the busy months of February and March.

Four people can be an ideal number for longer and more difficult trips, primarily for safety reasons. If one person is injured, two can go for help while the third person stays with the one who is injured. Some hut systems require a minimum of four people in order to reserve a hut.

Many of the smaller huts and most of the yurts accommodate from six to ten people, which makes it possible for groups this size to rent an entire cabin.

Larger groups can be a lot of fun. A group large enough to rent an entire cabin will enjoy having all the space to itself. Groups who book an entire cabin have more freedom with some of the cabin rules, such as when everyone needs to be quiet and where to sleep.

Keep in mind that large groups require considerably more planning than smaller ones. Large groups also travel more slowly. A good group leader is essential in keeping a large group organized.

CHECK YOUR ABILITY LEVEL, STRENGTH AND, ENDURANCE

Your group's ability level will determine which huts you'll choose. Always choose a hut based on the ability of the *weakest* member of your group. Don't try to push a slower member to keep up with the stronger travelers.

First-time hut users should choose cabins that are closest to the trailheads, require less difficult climbs, have minimal danger of avalanches, and offer routes which are easy to find. A well-marked trail is reassuring to the person traveling in the backcountry for the first time.

If members of your group lack proper equipment, encourage them to rent equipment a few days in advance so they can try it out, and be sure that it fits. Equipment failure is one of the most common reasons for slow moving groups. For more information on equipment, see Chapter 4, Gizmology.

Consider your potential and probable speed of travel when choosing your group. Mileage, difficult terrain, long climbs, problematic route-finding, or the need to break trail after fresh snowfall will affect your time on the trail.

If you are planning an ambitious hut trip, choose your group members accordingly. A strong group of well-seasoned backcountry travelers can reach the most difficult huts. They must have the strength, endurance, training, and ability to spend many hours on the trail carrying heavy loads. They should own their own equipment, know how it works, and know how to fix it. They should also have avalanche rescue gear such as transceivers and probes.

How Much Can You Carry?

Does your group have some strong work horses whom you can load down with extra food and drink? Lucky you. Put the heavier weights on the backs of the larger and stronger members to lighten the load for those less strong. Your group will then travel at a more even pace. A general rule is to carry no more than one third of your body weight. A woman weighing 110 pounds should carry less than a 170-pound man.

How Do You Travel?

Will your group be traveling on skis, snowshoes, or both? Skis are faster than snowshoes. With glide for every kick and the ability to coast down hills, skiers will quickly out-distance snowshoers. If your group is a mix of skiers and snowshoers, allow extra time for the snowshoers to get where you're going. People hauling sleds will move more slowly than their load-toting companions.

Group Compatibility

What is your group's primary interest in going to the hut? To hang out and relax? To tour or make as many ski turns as possible? To read and spend quiet time? To party and stay up late? When you put your group together, try to find people who want to do the same things. Don't put the speed demons with the slow-pokes, the slobs with the neat freaks, the partiers with the early risers.

Cross-country skiing to the huts with children. See Chapter 17, Children at the Huts for planning considerations. Photo by Maggie Lifland

SHOULD YOU HIRE A GUIDE?

If you're unsure of your group's ability, or if you want expert, worry-free planning, hire a guide.

The many services that guides offer more than justify their expense. They get you to the cabin, avoid hazards along the way, handle logistics, and feed and entertain you. Guides share information about animal tracks, vegetation, geology, and history of the area. They can tell you where the best ski runs are or where to find the most beautiful wildflowers. Guides will also take care of enforcing hut rules, equipment repair, and first aid.

Many guide services have storage lockers at the cabins stocked with sleeping bags, gear, wine, food, and other staples. That means you'll have less to carry. Most guide services that provide sleeping bags give you a bag liner to use during your stay.

There are many licensed outfitters or guides approved by the U.S. Forest Service to lead groups to the huts. They have undergone a lengthy screening process, are insured, and are required to show proof of medical, rescue, and avalanche training.

Beware of unlicensed guides. Some people pose as hut guides, but lack the insurance, and skills required to do a good job. Don't be afraid to ask for proof of insurance and a copy of their outfitter and guide permit from the U.S. Forest Service. For a list of outfitters and guides permitted to take guests to the hut you are interested in, ask the hut's reservations department.

Tips from Experienced Hut-Trippers

WHAT MAKES A GOOD GROUP LEADER
Someone who will warn the travelers behind him about the horse dung ahead.

WHAT MAKES A BAD GROUP LEADER
Sandy was flustered as she hurriedly packed for her first hut trip. She hoped she had everything as she rushed out the door, knowing she was already late for the rendezvous at the trailhead. The group leader greeted Sandy icily and quickly proceeded to corral the group and "finally" get on the trail. It was then that Sandy realized she had forgotten the climbing skins she had rented specifically for the trip. The group leader raised a terrible stink: "I'm not taking you people on this hut trip. It's too late and now we'll never get to the hut if we have to wait for Sandy." The group leader went home. Sandy was more determined than ever to get to the cabin. Her true friend offered to share climbing skins. With one ski gliding over the snow, and the other one sticking mightily as the climbing skin took hold, the two women made their way to the hut. They were rewarded with a wonderful hut experience and the deep personal satisfaction of rising to the challenge.

Choosing a Hut

A hut trip can be one of the finest adventures you'll ever have, and the hut you choose will be a large part of that adventure. In addition to the length of the trail, its difficulty and potential natural hazards, you must also consider the hut itself. What amenities does the hut have? How many people will the hut accommodate? What activities are available at the hut? Are the dates you want available, or is the hut already booked?

Each hut is different. Some characteristics depend on their location or the kind of skiing nearby. Others reflect the character of the person after whom they were named, or from people who built them. Others are special because of their remoteness. The newer huts tend to have bigger windows, more efficient cooking facilities, and technologically advanced photovoltaic systems. Some even have indoor, composting toilets. Older huts are more rustic, smaller, and cozy like a well-loved pair of old slippers.

TIPS FROM EXPERIENCED HUT-TRIPPERS

To really know how "to do a hut," you have to visit it first. Make a reconnaissance. Send a small group in advance for a quick overnight trip to get the lay of the land. Check out the routes. Get the timing down. Find the best ski terrain or hiking trails. Then go back for a longer stay or with a larger group of friends.

Janet's Cabin, Summit Huts Association system, Colorado. Photo by Pete Wingle

ACTIVITIES ONCE YOU GET THERE

All of the huts in the West offer the opportunity to ski in the general area of the hut. However, at some huts it takes a trained eye to identify those ski areas. Some huts have better skiing in the spring when snow cover is better and more stable than in mid-winter. But with a little exploring and a good eye for powder snow, you'll find that any cabin will provide memorable skiing. Lower-elevation huts may be better for touring and exploring. In the summer, you'll be hiking, peak climbing, fishing, mountain biking, bird watching, wildflower viewing, or just hanging out.

Hut Amenities

What kind of kitchen amenities a hut offers are an important consideration when making your reservation. Some cabins have woodburning stoves and propane cooktops but no ovens. Inquire before you carry that twenty pound, uncooked turkey into a cabin for Thanksgiving.

Other comforts may be important to your group. Find out if the cabin has photovoltaic lighting, indoor or outdoor toilets, private bedrooms, a well-stocked library, or any other "necessities" before making a reservation.

Motorized access is discouraged at most huts and is prohibited at many. Some cabins, however, permit snowmobiles. Many U.S. Forest Service fire lookouts and cabins in Montana are accessible by snowmobile. A few private cabins may also allow snowmobile support for your gear.

Making a Reservation

Before calling for a reservation, read the brochures. Meet with your group and assess your ability level. Then study maps to see what routes and which huts your group wants to tackle. Have an idea when you want to go but be flexible with your dates. After receipt of your payment, the reservations staff will send you a confirmation packet containing the combination lock number or the key to the cabin, the liability release forms, information about the hut, a recommended equipment list, parking passes, and other useful information.

The popularity of the hut and yurt systems has made it increasingly difficult to get special days reserved. Weekends, full moons, and three-day holidays are generally booked a year in advance. For assured reservations at the 10th Mountain and Summit Huts in Colorado, join the 10th Mountain Division Hut Association. TMDHA members can reserve huts beginning the first of April which gives them a two-month head start over the general public who can reserve huts for the next season only after

Tips from the Pros

Make sure the others in your group are committed to the trip. We've seen many people who make the reservations and pay the fee for the group get stuck holding the bill when their friends bail out at the last minute. Be sure to collect money up front.
—10th Mountain Division Hut Association reservation staff

March 1. The easiest months to get a reservation on short notice are December and April.

All hut systems have a cancellation policy. Check with the reservationist for details. Some huts give full refunds or exchange dates due to avalanche conditions or illness. Be sure to ask when making your reservation.

There are endless choices to make when deciding on a hut, yurt, fire

THE TOP 10 QUESTIONS THAT DRIVE A RESERVATIONIST CRAZY

1. *Is there a hot tub?*
2. *So, I just. . .what? Follow the signs up there?*
3. *You ski uphill to the huts?*
4. *Is there snow up there?*
5. *We have to pay?*
6. *Do they have TVs in the huts?*
7. *Can I plug my hair dryer into the photovoltaics?*
8. *Do the outhouses smell?*
9. *Climbing skins? What are those?*
10. *Do we need to bring food?*

Hidden Treasure Yurt near Edwards, Colorado, provides comfortable sleeping, eating, and cooking accommodations for up to eight people. Photo by Terri Thomas

lookout, or shelter. If you want to stay at a fully-catered cabin with meals, service, and staff the Appalachian Mountain Club cabins are for you.

If you want to get twenty or thirty miles into the backcountry with snow-mobile support, try the Montana cabins managed by the U.S. Forest Service.

If you've always been a winter camper and want to move up a step in comfort, try one of the numerous yurt systems sprinkled around the western United States.

If you'd like a helicopter trip into a remote cabin in the heart of Canada's glacier country, refer to the hut systems mentioned in Appendix B for the experience of a lifetime.

The flagship system in North America is the 10th Mountain Division Hut System, a series of semi-rustic cabins between Aspen and Vail, Colorado. This system enables you to do hut-to-hut tours, as well as make trips to individual huts with their numerous possibilities for skiing and sightseeing.

You will find a variety of people at the huts, ranging from first-time users to people who work ski patrols and have excellent backcountry knowledge. Talk to these people, and use the opportunity to advance your knowledge and skills about the backcountry. Keep your ears, eyes, and mind open. You will be amazed at how much you can learn that will make hut-to-hut trips even more enjoyable.

THINGS THAT GO BUMP IN THE NIGHT

I have slept on many hut trips in Europe, but it hasn't been easy. People are always getting up in the wee hours checking equipment, relieving themselves, getting ready for the next day's climb or ski. But at the Monchjoch Hütte in the Bernese Oberland, the couple next to me had amore on their minds. I was awakened first by whispers at 3:00 A.m., then never did get back to sleep through the rising crescendo of movement and muffled groans. At about 4:00 A.m. they finally dressed for their climb. Needless to say, I was vicariously spent as our group approached the same climb several hours later. My only consolation was that we passed a rather exhausted looking couple on our way to a successful climb to the summit of the Jungfrau.
    —John G. Warner, D.D.S.

GIZMOLOGY

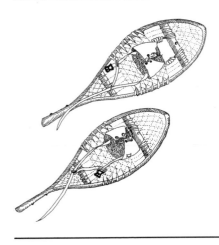

Beware of all enterprises
that require new clothes.
—*Henry David Thoreau*
(1817-1862)

When Thoreau wrote these words, the only option for backcountry clothing was wool in either dark gray or light gray. Today, new materials and new designs hit the market every year; some are flops, some are great. Gizmology is an evolving art.

Gizmology is a term coined by members of the Vail Ski Patrol to describe all the bells and whistles appearing on ski equipment in the early- to mid-1980s—and the art of repairing these bells and whistles when they broke. Since those days gizmology has gained a broader definition; it tends to include anything involved with winter sports, bicycles, or sports technology as we know it.

This chapter is a primer about gizmology and how it applies to hut trips. The time you spend in the backcountry will teach you more about specific gear, clothing, and how to be comfortable in even the worst of weather. Skiing and mountaineering are constantly evolving. The only constants are change and the increasing cost of equipment. It will take time and likely some trials and errors to figure out what equipment is for you. Take your time: shop, talk with more experienced skiers and climbers, and read.

Duct tape: the backcountry's fix-all. Photo by John Warner

HARDWARE

In the skiing world, hardware is equipment. It includes boots, skis, snowshoes, packs, and other gizmos that help you go. Hardware has become more durable, practical, and dependable over the years, and to some extent more user-friendly. There are four important points to keep in mind about equipment: It must fit you; you must know how to use it; it must be durable; and it must be easily repaireable in the field. Your boots should be comfortable and practical for the type of travel you plan. Skis should be the right length. Snowshoes must be the right size for the type of snow you'll be in–the deeper and softer the snow, the larger the snow-shoe surface-area should be. If you plan to take a snowboard, consider the type of snow you're likely to encounter. Snow in the backcountry is different from snow at ski areas.

Backcountry, winter hut travel requires either skis or snowshoes. You can use fat skis, skinny skis, metal snowshoes, wooden snowshoes, tele-mark skis, touring skis, racing snowshoes, or trekking snowshoes.

Twenty Backcountry Essentials

Following is a list of twenty essentials that everyone should carry with them when going into the backcountry.

1. Map
2. Compass
3. Flashlight/headlamp
4. Extra food
5. Extra clothing
6. Sunglasses
7. First aid supplies
8. Pocket-knife
9. Matches
10. Fire starter materials
11. Space Blanket
12. Three large, plastic leaf bags, to be used for rain and wind protection
13. Duct tape, enough to fix anything
14. Ensolite pad
15. Stove and pot
16. Whistle
17. Signal mirror
18. 100 feet of parachute cord
19. Toilet paper
20. Tool kit

Duct tape is an essential item—don't leave home without it!. You can use it to:

1. Patch torn clothing.
2. Keep ski probe poles from sliding down too far when skiing by wrapping the tape around the poles.
3. Rig a sled from skis for an emergency evacuation.
4. Stop down from leaking from your sleeping bag.
5. Tape heels to avoid blisters and hot spots.
6. Mark your coffee cup so you don't have to wash it after every use.
7. Identify which pot holds purified water.
8. Tape your boot to your ski when your binding breaks.
9. Tape your shovel to your boot when your ski breaks.
10. Tape your climbing skins to your skis.

TIPS FROM EXPERIENCED HUT-TRIPPERS

Must haves for a happy hut trip:

ear plugs

face cloth or bandanna

pillow case

moleskin for blisters

extra Ziploc bags

extra lip balm

hut slippers

Snowshoes

There are two forms of snowshoes: new-age metal and/or plastic shoes and the old-fashioned wood-framed, sinew-body shoes that have been around much longer than the huts. The new-style shoes made of light-weight, space-age metals and plastics have excellent binding systems that pivot under the ball of the foot and require less energy over a long trip than old lash-on bindings. New snowshoes also come with crampons under the foot to keep the snowshoes from slipping on sidehill trails, and on steeper ascents and descents. These new-age snowshoes come in a variety of sizes and styles. Larger snowshoes work best in deep, light snow because the larger surface keeps you closer to the surface of the snow so that you won't sink to your waist with each step. The small, lightweight shoes do well on packed trails and are good for running in snowshoe races. We don't recommended them for backcountry hut trips because they can't support the additional weight of a heavy pack.

The old-style wooden snowshoes look great with their hand-bent wooden frames and honey-colored finish, but unless they come with the hinged binding and crampons under the foot, they'll be hard to use in the field.

Skis

Not only do skis allow you to use gravity to your advantage, but, with cross-country bindings that enable you to lift your heel, you can also walk comfortably uphill. There are backcountry touring skis, telemark skis, and alpine touring or randonnée skis. Avoid lightweight skis, boots, and bindings designed for skiing at a nordic center. Those skis sacrifice durability, stability, and dependability to gain an advantage in weight. Skinny skis, light boots, a heavy pack, and a backcountry trail make a poor combination.

Skis with metal edges are a must for any backcountry hut trip because they provide greater control on steep descents, especially if the trail is hard-packed or icy.

Snowshoes are a popular way to get to the huts and yurts.
Photo by Gary Soles

Backcountry touring gear is lighter than its beefier cousin, telemark gear, and is best used for exactly what the name says: touring in the backcountry. These skis will have either a three-pin binding or a bar-and-latch system between the boot and binding. Three-pin bindings have three pins on the plate of the binding that fit into three corresponding holes in the sole of the ski boot and are held in place by a bail that clamps the boot to the binding. The term "pinheads" describing cross-country skiers refers to these bindings.

Backcountry touring gear is great for traveling to and from the huts, but it is not good for extended days of telemark skiing or steep and tricky descents. Lighter-weight boots are not as sturdy or as warm as a heavier boot. A Super Gaitor used with lighter-weight boots can add ten degrees of warmth to your feet.

Cross-country skis vary from thin and light to fat and beefy.
Photo by Brian Litz

Telemark skiing requires wider skis, stiffer boots with greater ankle support, and heavy-duty cable and/or three-pin bindings. Many three-pin bindings can be fitted with a cable that wraps around the boot heel to provide more torsional stability for telemark turns. Paul Parker, author of *Free-Heel Skiing*, offers brief instruction on learning the telemark turn in Chapter 10, At the Hut.

Alpine touring gear, also known as AT or randonnée, is another option for backcountry skiing. AT boots are made of plastic and resemble downhill ski boots, except that they are softer for more comfortable climbing, and their downhill performance is slightly inferior to a downhill boot. The AT binding allows the heel to lift for uphill skiing and can be latched to

Randonnée equipment allows for easier crossover from ski area to backcountry skiing. Photo by Brian Litz

A simple way to transform your alpine ski equipment into randonnée equipment is the Alpine Trekker bindings insert that allows for free-heel walking. Photo by Bruce Edgerly

the heel for parallel-turn descents. Some AT systems are lighter than telemark equipment. Of course this equipment comes at a price, and a high one at that.

Remember, stiffer skis, boots, and beefier bindings add weight to your feet. Every pound added to your feet is like adding ten pounds to your pack. This added weight makes for greater reliability and durability in the backcountry, however. Heavier boots are usually warmer, but they also require more break-in time than the lighter touring boot.

Repair Kit

Once you've decided on your means of transportation, put together your repair kit. Include appropriate spare parts for bindings, packs and boots, and all needed tools. You should be able to repair or replace ski pole parts and baskets, as well as splint a broken pole. Duct tape could be one of the most valuable items in your kit, for it can temporarily fix just about anything. See Appendix E, Equipment List, for more suggestions on what to include in your repair kit.

A variety of boots are available for backcountry use. Photo by Leigh Girvin Yule

Repair kits should contain tools and materials to fix your equipment.
Photo by Leigh Girvin Yule

Backpacks

Backpacks are another form of hardware, and are as important as your skis, boots, and bindings. You'll be carrying a large load on your back while skiing up and down hills. A well-fitted pack can make all the difference between flailing hopelessly down a narrow, steep, tree-lined descent, or comfortably negotiating your way through variable snow conditions. The best packs for hut trips have an internal frame that fits closely to your body. Be sure its length is appropriate for your height so that the pack sits comfortably on your hips. You don't want the hip belt to cut into your stomach. A padded hip belt and padded shoulder and chest straps are important considerations as well. Unless you're going on a very short hut trip, don't use your external frame backpack. While it's cooler in summer, it sits away from your body and will cause problems with balance.

To find the best pack for you, shop around and try on on as many different packs as you can. Borrow a friend's pack for a day and try it out. It's always a good idea to try the pack fully loaded for an idea of how it feels with weight.

Sleds

A sled gets the weight off your shoulders and allows you to carry more gear, and even children. On a level trail, without sidehills, a sled works well. If the terrain falls off to the side, however, sleds can slip sideways or tip over. A simple cure for sled-sliding is the use of a tail rope. A tail rope is used by a second person to keep the back of the sled from slipping or tipping over. Some people choose to have every member of the group carry a light pack in addition to using a sled for food and heavy items. Each person can take a turn pulling the sled. When skiing a sled downhill, you must use caution and control your speed.

Sleds can be used to carry just about everything.
Photo by Scott Toepfer

TIPS FROM EXPERIENCED HUT-TRIPPERS

Access to sunscreen, water, snacks, and your camera is difficult when these items are packed in the sled. Wear a small fanny pack to keep these items handy.

Author Leigh Girvin Yule, with knee pads on, takes a break. Photo by John Warner

Knee Pads

Knee pads are one of the most important pieces of hardware a telemark skier can purchase. Knee pads help protect the kneecap and femur during telemark turns. Tele-skiers should never venture into the backcountry without their knee pads on.

Avalanche Equipment

Winter travel in the backcountry almost always involves passing through avalanche terrain. Not only will you need appropriate and reliable equipment you'll need to know how to use it. Brains, beacons, shovels, slope meters, and probe poles are essential avalanche equipment.

Beacons are worthless if you don't know how to use them. Practice setting the beacons and interpreting the beeps before you head out. Only transceivers on the new 457 khz universal standard should be used.

Shovels are essential and have many uses. You can dig snow shelters, tape to your boot if you break a ski or snowshoe, uncover your car at the trailhead, get snow to melt for water—and they are indispensable for digging people out of avalanche debris.

A slope meter shows the angle of a slope so you'll know if you're in avalanche terrain. These devices are inexpensive and lightweight and can be carried in a shirt pocket or side pouch. More on this subject in Chapter 7, Natural Hazards.

Getting Uphill

You can go uphill with skis three different ways, with fish scales, wax, or climbing skins. Fish-scale skis have engravings on the bottom that resemble fish scales. These engravings grip the snow and allow you to walk uphill. They do not allow for good glide, however, and consequently are not the best for extended downhills or telemark turns. They also may not grip on steep uphill slopes.

There are two types of ski wax, glide wax for gliding and kick wax for climbing. World Cup cross-country ski racers looking for the perfect combination of kick and glide spend hours mixing waxes for the competitive advantage. Hut skiers will find that following the directions on the back of the wax can will usually be good enough for their use.

Ski wax is designed for different snow temperatures and types of snow. You'll need a variety of waxes for different weather conditions. Most skiers use a cork to rub the wax into a wax pocket under the foot. For hut trips with a heavy pack you'll want to apply wax the full length of the ski to maximize grip on slopes. The wax that is good for gripping will reduce downhill glide, so bring along a scraper, too.

Climbing skins can also get you uphill. Ski wax and fish-scale skis work well in some situations, but the best way to get up a long, steep hill on skis is with a pair of ski skins. Ski skins can be made of plastic, nylon, or mohair. Plastic skins are the cheapest. They strap to your skis and are easy to put on and take off. They also require minimum maintenance and care. They climb well but provide very little glide on downhill sections or flat terrain.

Nylon and mohair have their advantages. Nylon skins are more durable, which is important if you plan to use skins in the spring when the snow is abrasive. Nylon skins don't glide as well as mohair skins but are better than plastic. Mohair glides much better than nylon or plastic, but wears out faster, too.

Nylon and mohair skins come with one of two modes of attachment. They either glue to the bottom of the ski or strap on. Glue-on skins have the advantage that snow can't build up between the ski and the climbing skin. When breaking trail through deep powder, however, the skin can pull off the bottom of the ski and may be difficult to reattach. Whenever you remove your skins for a run, fold them carefully and place them near your body so the glue stays warm and supple.

With glue-on skins you can avoid the aggravating little slip between the ski and the skin before the skin takes hold on the snow. Glue-on skins require careful attention. If dirt, hair, or lint gets on the glue, the skins won't stick. Skins should also be air dried after each use. An easy way to dry skins is to hang them from the ceiling (away from the cat). Eventually skins may need to be reglued, a procedure that can be done at any reputable ski shop.

TIPS FROM EXPERIENCED HUT-TRIPPERS

To keep your glue-on skins warm and supple, store them inside your jacket and tucked partially into the waistband of your pants. Or, if you have an internal gaiter on your ski pants, slip them between the internal gaiter and your boots.

Removing climbing skins for the descent. Photo by Scott Toepfer

Sleeping Bags

Since temperatures inside the hut can reach into the seventies, it's unecessary to bring a heavy sleeping bag good to -45°F. A sleeping bag with a temperature rating of 5 to 20°F will work best in the hut, and will also be sufficient if you get stuck in a snowcave overnight. Another handy item for out-of-hut- survival is a bivouac sack. Small and lightweight, bivy sacks act as personal tents and add several degrees of warmth to your bag's temperature rating.

Headlamps

Look for a headlamp that is comfortable on your head for long periods of time. Headlamps are handy if the solar lighting system in the hut goes out, for overnight bivouacs along the trail, and to keep your hands free for other things.

SOFTWARE

As hardware is equipment, software is clothing, and clothing has become warmer, lighter, and remains dryer under wetter conditions than it did before. Even in these days of high technology, wool remains one of the best fabrics to keep your body dry and warm. Its main drawbacks are its weight, bulk, and the fact that it retains water.

Modern chemistry has given us new synthetic fabrics that have increased efficiency, comfort, and practicality for backcountry users; but these synthetics aren't cheap. They may also give people a false sense of security in the backcountry. Backcountry travelers must always remember that it is our skill and not our gear that gets us where we want to go.

When you think about clothing, consider the climate you'll be in and wether it's wet or dry. Colorado has a dry climate; the Pacific Northwest is wet. Avoid down products in a wet climate, and consider using the new fiberfill products for clothing and sleeping bags. Always dress in layers. You must be able to remove a layer of clothing easily when you get too warm and add a layer as soon as you get cold.

One of the simple joys in backcountry travel is having dry socks. Try to fit in an extra two pair for any overnight trip: a pair of lightweight polypropylene or nylon socks and a pair of heavy wool socks. If you start to feel a hot spot on your foot, change into dry socks.

Many additional items fit our definition of gizmology and are covered in Appendix E. Be sure to consult the equipment and survival kit lists.

DRESSING FOR A HUT TRIP

A primer by John Cooley, Marmot Mountain Ltd.

The best approach I've found for dressing comfortably and properly for a Colorado hut trip is to visualize both the warmest and the coldest conditions I'm likely to encounter, and then pack accordingly. Blizzard conditions at 11,000 feet with low temperatures, high winds, low visibility, and drifting snow are as likely as alpine touring through gentle glades on one of Colorado's 300 plus days of sunshine. Picture yourself in each condition; mentally dress yourself from head to toe and then pack quickly before you forget.

With that said, the most common mistake is packing too much. You need to stay warm, but you also need to stay lightweight. Speed and endurance can be more important than warmth. You must strike a reasonable balance between the two.

A Simple Clothing System

Layering is a buzzword that simply means you dress from the inside out with lightweight garments that fit over one another. A simple clothing system would consist of: 1) a wicking layer; 2) an insulating layer; and 3) a windproof shell layer.

Wicking Layer

A wicking layer ventilates the skin to keep it cool and transports moisture away to keep it relatively dry. Modern base-layer textiles do not absorb moisture that will chill you when you stop to rest or read a map. Cotton T-shirts are not appropriate. Light-colored base layers show dirt more easily but will be more comfortable on hot, sunny days. Most base-layer textiles are synthetics that can be washed and dry quickly overnight. They also melt easily, so be careful of the stove.

Insulating Layer

An insulating middle layer traps tiny pockets of stable air that your body heats up to keep you warm. The thicker the pockets of trapped air, the greater the insulation. But one thick layer does not provide the versatility of adjustment that multiple layers do. I carry two insulating garments: a fleece sweater and a down (or synthetic-fill) sweater. I never use the down sweater unless I am stopped; it is my insurance policy. Start the day cold; you'll warm up soon enough.

Shell Layer

The outside layer of your clothing system should be windproof, waterproof, ventable, breathable, and lightweight. Again, modern textiles provide ultralight, high performance alternatives. Gore-Tex ® fabric outerwear is the best known, best performing, and the most durable choice mountaineering outerwear. Lined jackets are heavier than unlined jackets. Insulated downhill ski outerwear is likely too heavy to be appropriate for a hut trip. An unlined, three-layer Gore-Tex fabric, hooded jacket is an easy way to save weight; full performance models weigh as little as 18 ounces! Make sure your shell clothing fits over all your inner layers, allows free and easy movement when reaching and stretching, has plenty of pockets, and is easy to use. Full side-zip shell pants are more convenient than pull-on styles. Bring waterproof gaiters.

Odds and Ends

I carry three hats: a long brimmed sun hat, an ordinary ski hat, and a windproof hat that covers my ears. My shell jacket always has a neoprene face mask zipped into a pocket. I have two pairs of gloves: warm weather and cold weather. Don't forget that your hands can get sunburned too. Keep sunglasses and yellow-lens goggles in your top pocket.

Hut Wear

Plan to step out of all your clothes when you hit the hut. Likely your clothes will be wet; in any event, you'll be more comfortable. Lightweight fleece pants or tights are great for hut bottoms. I use a cotton T and my down sweater on top. Down booties, heavy socks or slippers are fine inside, but remember they will be slippery if you go outside to see the stars. I try to remember to bring a small hand towel. It is always amazing how many streams, saunas, and hand showers you'll find along the way.

5

GETTING READY

It has long been an axiom of mine that the little things are infinitely the most important.
—*Sir Arthur Conan Doyle*
(1859-1930)

Getting ready for a hut trip involves three things: careful planning, getting in shape, and organizing your equipment. Share ideas, help each other, develop trust, and you're well on your way to a successful trip.

PLANNING YOUR TRIP

Once your group has decided on a hut, you need to plan the details of the trip. A group meeting is an important part of the process, so schedule a meeting when everyone can attend. When you're in the expedition planning room, make sure you cover the following:

- Choose a group leader.
- Familiarize everyone with the information packet you'll receive along with your hut confirmation letter. Distribute copies to group members.
- Discuss what gear each member of the group will need.
- Have everyone go over the maps and know the route.
- Establish roles and responsibilities for each group member.
- Plan meals with special consideration given to food allergies and preferences.
- Decide who will carry what communal items.
- Give everyone the hut combination or designate a key holder.

- Designate someone to call the avalanche and weather hotline before the trip.
- Establish an itinerary for the trip.
- Organize a carpool if necessary.
- Find out if you need a four-wheel-drive to get to the trailhead.
- Sign and initial release forms.

Develop and discuss an emergency plan. Never assume you'll make it to your destination. Make sure everyone has the appropriate survival gear in case you have to camp outdoors. Survival techniques are discussed in Chapter 9, Not Getting There.

If you work the details out well in advance of the trip, you'll save yourselves a lot of trouble at the trailhead. Tell everyone to call the trip organizer if anything seems amiss, or if any questions arise about who is responsible for what part of the trip.

GET IN SHAPE

You'll do best on your hut trip if you have good aerobic capacity, strong legs and back, and long-distance endurance. Several activities can get you into shape for a hut trip. Cross-country skiing or snowshoeing with a heavy pack are the best. If you're planning a trip requiring a long ski or

All members of an expedition study the maps. Photo by Leigh Girvin Yule

snowshoe, build up your endurance over time. Ski or snowshoe shorter distances on several outings and work up to longer distances until you're comfortable covering the same distance as your trip.

If you live in a warm climate and can't ski, cross-train by running, cycling, or doing aerobics. These exercises are excellent for building strength for cross-country skiing. Look for programs that work lungs, legs, and shoulders.

GET ACCLIMATED

It's important that you acclimate to altitude before you begin your trip. Many western huts are at elevations above 11,000 feet—more than twice as high as Denver, Colorado. If you're traveling from sea level, plan to stay a night or two at gradually higher elevations to help you get used to the altitude. If you've had problems with altitude in the past, talk to your physician about taking Diamox, a prescription drug that helps alleviate altitude sickness symptoms. Techniques for adjusting to altitude and altitude sickness are covered in Chapter 14, To Your Health, and Chapter 15, First Aid and Rescue.

Heading into Gothic Cabin below, Gothic Peak, near Crested Butte, Colorado.
Photo by Scott Toepfer

ORGANIZE YOUR EQUIPMENT

Begin by setting everything you plan to take with you on the floor. Place hand, head, and foot gear in one pile, toilet articles in another, jackets and shirts in another. Then start taking away the things you don't really need. The art of packing is in not bringing too much.

Pack from the bottom of your pack to the top. The sleeping bag goes first, then put in your hut clothes and survival gear. On top go the things you need on the trail.

Assorted nylon stuff sacks work well for organizing gear. Put meals in one bag and clothes in another. Ziploc bags work well for cameras, toiletries, and lunches. Put water bottles, baseball caps, and sunglasses in an accessible place on the outside of your pack. Repair kits, sunscreen, and stoves go in outside pack pouches. Keep your toothbrush and stove fuel in different pouches or you may not want to brush your teeth.

An eighty five pound backpack and still smiling.
Photo by Scott Toepfer

6

BACKCOUNTRY ETHICS, ETIQUETTE, AND PROTOCOL

When things are steep, remember to
stay level-headed.
—Quintus Horatius Flaccus, (65-8B.C.)

The understanding and practice of backcountry ethics is an essential aspect of learning to travel and operate there.

TREAD LIGHTLY AND TAKE OUT WHAT YOU BRING IN

Tread lightly and leave no trace. Only if we travel with this care and consciousness can we hope that our children and grandchildren will have the opportunity to enjoy the mountains as we do. Winter snow may hide many abuses of the mountains, but when the snow recedes in spring, we see the impact of our presence.

It's unusual these days not to come upon other people's trash. Inconsiderate winter users leave duct tape, broken ski poles, toilet paper, and gum wrappers behind them. The responsible backcountry traveler packs out absolutely everything he or she packs in—and even packs out other people's trash when necessary.

Erosion from vehicles, horses, bikes, and boots is also evident in summer when the fragile soil is exposed to view. Walking through the fragile meadows and wetlands can cause erosion. Stay on designated trails. Don't short-cut switchbacks, since doing so increases erosion and washes out trails. When you take a rest, snack, or lunch break, find a rock or downed-log to stand or sit on. That way you will have less impact on fragile ground or vegetation.

Mountain bikes on wet earth can be devastating, so if you ride a bike, stay on the designated trails. Never ride across meadows, alpine tundra, or on wet trails.

Flush toilets aren't one of the conveniences of backcountry travel. Bury your excrement in at least six inches of soil. Keep the used toilet paper in your own plastic bag and make sure you pack it out with you. Never leave toilet paper along the trail, behind a tree, under a rock, or buried. Doing so is like leaving your used toilet paper littered throughout someone else's house. In winter, hide evidence of your presence by relieving yourself away from the trail so that other travelers aren't confronted by your stain. Remember, you are a traveler passing through the backcountry. Love it, respect it, and care for it. Kathleen Meyer's *How to Shit in the Woods* is an indispensable guide for any backcountry traveler.

ETIQUETTE AND PROTOCOL

Skiers in the Elk Range, Colorado. Photo by Scott Toepfer

Billy Mattison of the Vail Ski Patrol developed these lists for backcountry etiquette and protocol:

Etiquette

1. Know your partner(s).
   - Don't press people beyond their limits.
   - Know their skills, gear, and knowledge.
2. Keep your exploits quiet.
   - Don't brag about your assumed prowess.
   - Don't make your powder stashes a public "secret;" the fewer people skiing, the fewer accidents for search and rescue.
3. Help others.
   - Suggest a safe route.
   - Suggest taking an avalanche course.
4. Help the experienced.
   - Keep your eyes and ears open; you may be called on to help someone in trouble.
5. Call the local avalanche center with any avalanche data.
   - Recent slides (witnessed).
   - Snow-pit data.
6. Know your backcountry ethics.
   - Pack it in and pack it out.
   - Don't be loud.
7. Conserve natural resources.
   - Keep your ski tracks close together.
   - Save untracked snow for the next group.
   - Try not to cross other people's tracks when making turns.

Protocol

Avalanche knowledge, survival craft, and good outdoor skills are more precious than gold in a winter mountain environment. All members of your group should have basic avalanche skills. It will do the knowledgeable leaders no good to get buried in an avalanche and expect someone with no avalanche skills to perform a successful rescue.

You'll want to develop your own standard operating procedures for traveling in the backcountry. Here are some ideas:

1. Let a responsible person know where, for how long, and with whom you will be traveling.
2. Don't travel alone in the backcountry. What might have been a minor incident with partners can be a disaster for a person traveling alone.

3. Carry the proper gear and check it all before leaving.
   - Shovel
   - Beacon
   - Slope meter
   - First aid and repair kits
4. Call the local avalanche hotline for information on conditions (See Appendix C).
5. Have good backcountry skills.
   - Practice with your beacon
   - Be a good skier
   - Be fit
   - Keep your speed under control
6. Know the weather conditions.
   - Route conditions
   - Past weather and forecasts
7. Find escape routes from avalanches.
   - Trees to hide behind
   - Cliff bands
   - Schuss to flanks
8. Ski across possible avalanche slopes one at a time.
   - Wait until skiers are in a safe spot.
   - Expose only one person at a time to danger.
9. Decide on communication signals such as poles in the air or whistles.

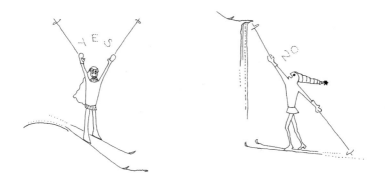

10. Wear bright colored clothing and gear because you're easier to spot in avalanche debris or on gray, cloudy days.
11. Keep the group together. Accidents happen on easy terrain.
12. Get an early start.

Backcountry education is the best way to prepare for backcountry adventure. A number of courses in backcountry use and survival are

Figure 8's are a great way to conserve untracked powder for the next skier. Photo by Scott Toepfer

offered every winter. Check with a local mountaineering store or the local avalanche forecast center for a list of classes in your area. All the book-smarts in the world will not substitute for practical experience, however. Reputable classes with plenty of field time are best.

People who are unprepared for danger and who have poor or under-developed outdoor skills can endanger other groups and rescuers. Proper backcountry skills and the knowledge and practice of backcountry ethics are essential for any group's safety and enjoyment.

Above timberline there are few landmarks but the mountains themselves.
Photo by Scott Toepfer

NATURAL HAZARDS

Education teaches the rules;
experience teaches the exceptions.
—Avalanche Awareness: A Question
of Balance, *1988 video*

Mother Nature displays her power in many ways, sometimes in the beauty of a sunset or a crystal clear, blue-sky day. Sometimes her power can be devastating to humans. Everyday natural occurrences are potential hazards for backcountry travelers. Avalanches pose a serious threat in winter and spring. Wild animals can be dangerous, although they generally try to avoid people. Lightning can strike in almost any season. Wildfires are a concern during dry months and in periods of drought. Most weather-related natural hazards can be avoided by being aware of what is going on around you. Learn to read the warning signs that Mother Nature broadcasts and learn how to act in a safe and rational manner.

For frequent backcountry users, the weather and what it does dictates the day. Weather determines where or if you go, what route to take, and what to bring. Any worthy backcountry "salt" starts a winter tour with a call to the local avalanche hotline for an avalanche and mountain weather forecast. Some states provide this service to the public from November to April. If your area is fortunate enough to have this service, it can be a great source of information.

AVALANCHES

The first thing to understand about avalanches, and other natural hazards, is that there are exceptions to every rule. A general rule of thumb states that the majority of avalanches run during or within twenty four hours after a storm. The trouble with this rule is that even a minority of avalanches can hurt or kill you. Ron Perla, a respected avalanche hand, has his own rule: There are no rules of thumb with regard to avalanches. Backcountry travelers need to educate themselves about avalanches. Before a hut trip, take a class which offers time in the field.

Four ingredients are required for an avalanche: a mountainside with a slope of twenty five degrees or more, snowpack with a slab or cohesive layer of snow, a weak layer in the snowpack or at the groundlevel which can cause the slab to come down, and a trigger, which frequently can be the weight of a backcountry traveler. There is no current technology or instrument to determine if snowpack is safe or not. Avalanche forecasting is as much an art as it is a science. To illustrate, we share with you the opening paragraph on avalanche forecasting from *The Avalanche Handbook:* Conventional avalanche forecasting refers to prediction of current and future snow stability by means of information and data from diverse sources largely without the aid of analytical techniques (formal numerical systems) or encoded symbolic logic (e.g., expert systems). In practice, conventional forecasting consists of assimilating the relevant information (measurements, observations, weather forecast) and using it to formulate a forecast based on experience, intuition, and local knowledge of the mountain range. Quite a mouthful, isn't it?

More than 80 percent of fatal avalanche accidents occur during backcountry travel. In the majority of these cases the victim or victims trigger the avalanche themselves. Winter backcountry travelers who head out thinking about avalanches are much less likely to trigger one and to suffer the consequences.

Practice identifying avalanche conditions based on the three elements of the avalanche-data triad: terrain, snowpack, and weather. The most important terrain feature that contributes to an avalanche is slope angle. Some 95 percent of avalanches release on terrain from 25 to 50 degrees in steepness in the starting zone. Avalanches are rare when the terrain you are on and the terrain immediately above you do not have slopes of this angle. The easiest and safest way to determine slope angle is to buy a slope meter, which, along with a shovel and avalanche transceivers, is an essential tool in your backcountry survival kit.

Avalanche equipment includes shovels, a slope meter, and transceivers or avalanche beacons. Photo by Leigh Girvin Yule

Remember that no slope has a constant thirty-degree pitch—all slopes have varying degrees of steepness. Find an area that is representative of the whole slope and find an "average" slope angle. Use this information to identify potential avalanche start-zones.

Snowpack and weather are more complicated aspects of the data triad and require a higher level of skill and experience to interpret and understand. The snowpack in a continental climate, such as that of Colorado, is generally shallow with cold temperatures at the surface of the snow and warmer temperatures at the ground. This sets up a temperature gradient, a difference in temperature between the ground and the surface of the snowpack. These differences between temperatures can result in a snowpack that can remain unstable for long periods of time—something for which Colorado is famous. A maritime climate, such as that of British Columbia or California, tends to create a more stable snowpack. Avalanches in a maritime climate are more predictable and tend to occur during or soon after a snow or rain event.

Dig a snow pit all the way to the ground and look closely at the different textures of snow. You will see a history of the current winter's snowfall, almost like a layer cake. As we all know, some layer cakes are better than others. Likewise, some snowpacks are better and safer than others. Now "taste" or test these different snowpack layers and see how they "digest". Use your shovel for shovel shear tests, Rutschblock tests, compression tests, or weighted column tests. Use your gloved hand to feel or "tweak" the snow. How does it react? Where are the weak layers? Use your ski pole to punch through the layers of snow. Are some layers stiffer than others? Use this information to help you determine if the slab can slide.

Snowpit data is part of the formula to determine if the snowpack is stable
Photo by Scott Toepler

Weather is the architect of avalanches. The most important weather question to ask is: Is the potential for avalanches increasing because of the weather? A change in the weather can increase the avalanche hazard in less than an hour. Watch for storms that produce an inch of snow or more per hour. Or storms with winds over fifteen miles per hour which can more than double the snowfall rate onto lee slopes. When winds over fifteen miles per hour combine with a snowfall from two to six inches, a slab can quickly build to one foot or more.

Keep a weather-eye out for other conditions. Pay attention to the sky cover and the types of clouds that indicate low pressure and incoming storms. Be aware of precipitation type, how much is falling, and how fast. Learn how to determine wind direction and speed. Measure temperature changes. If it is above or below freezing you can expect different kinds of avalanches—wet-slab, hard-slab, or soft-slab avalanches.

GOLDEN RULES

Now that you are practicing the art of avalanche forecasting, how do you travel safely in the backcountry? There are six golden rules to back-country travel: (1) educate yourself; (2) carry the right tools; (3) expose one person at a time to potential danger; (4) unburden yourself; (5) have escape routes; and select safe routes.

Educate Yourself

The most important rule is to learn about avalanches and safe winter travel through a reputable course that offers plenty of field experience. Don't ever feel you know it all. Avalanches will surprise you. Anticipate danger when you travel. Always ask yourself: Is this slope be safe to ski? Develop avalanche eyes.

Carry the Right Tools

In Chapter 4, Gizmology, we discussed avalanche tools. Know how to use your tools. The time to learn about your beacon, shovel, slope meter, or avalanche ski-pole probes is in the comfort of your own home, not in a howling blizzard while your best friend is buried under four feet of avalanche debris. The next time you go to a hut, have a beacon contest where you rescue the beacon. Team up in pairs, bury a beacon, and see how long it takes each person to retrieve it. Combine each team's time. The team taking longest to find the beacon washes dishes. Make it fun, but take it seriously. Practice, practice, practice!

One at a Time

Always expose only one person at a time to terrain capable of producing or being overrun by avalanches. Don't bunch up. It is much better to have six people looking for one buried person, than one looking for six buried. Stop only in safe spots and keep an eye on the skier on the avalanche slope. Develop hand signals in case you can't hear each other. A simple set of universal signals can be found in Chapter 6, Backcountry Ethics and Protocol.

Unburden Yourself

When traveling in avalanche-prone terrain, remove ski pole straps from your wrists and loosen or unbuckle waist belts on heavy packs. This is vital—if you are caught in an avalanche, you need to be able to ditch your gear so that it doesn't drag you down.

Have Escape Routes

Escape routes are places that you can easily reach to allow an avalanche to go by without you in it. These can be anything that divert the flow of an avalanche such as large rock outcrops, dense stands of timber, or ridges.

What is considered to be a safe distance between skiers depends on the terrain.
Photo by Scott Toepfer

Select Safe Routes

The safest place to be in an avalanche is near the starting area, or off to the side where you can more easily escape. When selecting a safe route, consider where you could be carried if the slope avalanches. Would you be swept over a cliff, into thick timber, or into a gully? Debris flowing into a gully can be very deep, and no one has been found alive when buried deeper than seven feet.

For most hut systems the designated routes avoid avalanche terrain as much as possible. Some routes, however, have pockets of avalanche terrain, and avalanches have run across trails. Hut trippers need to continually evaluate the terrain, the weather, and the snowpack throughout the trip. Conditions going to the hut may be different from conditions going out.

*The slope provides clues about where avalanches are
likely to occur. Photo by Scott Toepfer*

FROM THE LOGBOOK

Our first hut trip since taking the avalanche awareness course. Today we ski, build a snow pit, and do beacon searches. Yesterday, Martha showed us how to make a snow cave—very impressive. Last night Martha slept in her new snow cave and will be giving house tours this morning.

SUMMER CONCERNS

Thunder and Lightning

The finest thunder is found in the mountains. The crashing, booming, echoes and reverberations are the most awesome in a high mountain valley. These storms can also be the most dangerous. Lightning is one of Mother Nature's greatest threats. There are some forty million lightning strikes in the United States every year, killing, on average, nearly one hundred people. Colorado is second only to Florida in lightning strikes.

As mountain travelers we must first recognize potentially dangerous situations. All thunderstorms produce lightning. In summer, afternoon thunderstorms are common in mountain areas. There are three necessary ingredients for thunderstorms: moisture, atmospheric instability, and a trigger. Moisture provides the energy that drives thunderstorms (when water vapor condenses into droplets, it produces heat). Atmospheric instability occurs when a parcel of air rises from ground level to tens of thousands of feet. The only way this can happen is if the rising air is warmer than the surrounding atmosphere and therefore has buoyancy to continue its ascent. The trigger for thunderstorms is usually a lifting mechanism such as air heated by the sunlit ground underneath (thermals), cold fronts forcing warmer air to rise, or mountains which force air to climb to higher altitudes.

As moist air rises, it expands and cools. Eventually it condenses its moisture into droplets and or ice particles, forming a cloud. If it continues to rise it forms towering cumulus clouds which can rise tens of thousands of feet.

Vertical currents within cumulus clouds carry small droplets of water higher into the clouds. As these droplets and ice particles collide, electrical charges are generated within the cumulus cloud.

Air currents within the cloud distribute a strong negative charge near the base of the thunderhead. As the cloud moves along, the negative charge causes a positive charge to build at the ground. This positive charge will be found on all objects underneath the negatively-charged cloud base. Isolated objects that stick up above the earth's surface are spots where positive charges can build even more. Air is a fairly poor electrical conductor, but when the difference between the charges grows and exceeds the resistance in air, we see cloud-to-ground lightning. Sometimes people can actually feel and smell this electrical charge coming. The hair on the head and arms will stand. Some people say they can smell ozone before a strike. Static electricity will sometimes crackle around you. The average thunderstorm produces around 250 million watts of electricity. A large supermarket can consume 400,000 watts in the same time frame. Imagine the power of the average storm!

Fifty percent of all known lightning casualties occur on mountain summits, under a lone tree, in wide-open areas, and on lakes. If you find yourself in the path of an approaching thunderstorm, do the following:

- Get off ridges and peaks. Do not hide in a shallow cave or depression since electricity can arc across the opening like a spark plug.
- Avoid standing upslope from local terrain features such as rock outcrops and trees.
- If you are in a forest, seek shelter in low spots. If possible, crouch under a thick growth of small trees.
- If you are caught on open slopes, get down into a valley or canyon, but beware of flash floods.
- If you are camping in a tent on a bare slope or ridge, seek shelter in your car or in the forest.
- If none of these safety options are available, and you start to feel your skin tingle and your hair stand on end, lightning may be ready to strike. Drop to your knees and bend forward; place your hands on your knees. Do not lie flat because in this position an electrical current from a strike will more easily travel through vital organs.

First aid for lightning victims must be administered quickly. People who have been struck by lightning do not carry an electrical charge and can be handled safely. If the victim is not breathing, start mouth-to-mouth resuscitation. If there is no pulse, start cardiopulmonary resuscitation (CPR). In all cases, shock and burns are to be expected. Anyone struck by lightning will need to see a doctor. Evacuate the victim as quickly as possible. And remember that lightning can strike in winter, too.

Wildfire

Wildfires play a natural role in mountain ecology. It is the way forests are renewed. Wildfires can be a concern at the huts, especially in the summer and fall. The following guidelines will help your chances for survival if you are trapped in the backcountry by wildfire:

- Wear long pants and boots of natural fibers, not synthetics.
- Carry a long-sleeve shirt or jacket, gloves, a handkerchief to shield your

face, water to wet it, and goggles.
- Place large trash cans and buckets around the outside of the cabin and fill them with water.
- Soak rugs and rags with water to beat out burning embers or small fires.
- Remove any combustible items from around the cabin.
- If you are near a road, lie face down along the road or the ditch on the uphill side.
- Cover yourself with anything that will shield you from the fire's heat.
- Seek a depression with sparse fuel. Clear any fuel from the area while the fire is approaching and then lie face down in the depression and cover yourself.
- On a steep mountainside, the side away from an approaching fire is safest.
- Keep calm and let the fire pass.
- Avoid canyons and saddles along ridges. These are natural paths for fire winds.

In general the cabins are the safest place to be in the event of a fire, especially the large, log cabins. Most cabins have a defensible space around them. Trees and underbrush have been cleared from around the cabin so that it is more difficult for a fire to reach it. Some cabins are equiped with rakes, shovels, mattox, and other fire-fighting tools. If the cabin catches fire, move to an open, sparsely fueled area.

Consult the public agency which manages the area you will be traveling in for the current level of fire danger and for other tips on fire survival.

Wild Animals and Safety Tips

Humans and huts are the unnatural elements in the backcountry. Wild animals are the permanent residents there. Show respect for the animals. You are unlikely to have an unpleasant encounter if you don't stalk, feed, or chase the animals.

Bears are common in the mountain ranges where huts have been built. Though not as common, mountain lions have also been seen in the same areas. Both of these animals are potentially dangerous, so avoid doing anything that might attract them. Never leave food around the outside of a hut. Be especially aware at dawn, dusk, and dark when these animals are most active.

Other animals bear consideration. Elk and moose during the fall rut will become aggressive and should be given wide berth. Porcupines are more of a pest than a hazard. Porcupines love to gnaw on anything salty, such as boots or backpacks. Keep these items out of their reach. At times porcupines will even gnaw on the cabins, which can be disconcerting at two o'clock in the morning. If a porcupine is chewing on the cabin, throw a bucket of water on it and it'll quickly depart.

Natural hazards in the mountain backcountry are not to be taken lightly. But if you treat potential backcountry hazards with respect and practice good travel habits, you'll have adventures and stories to share on your next hut trip.

Mountain Lion Safety

- Keep children near you in the backcountry.
- Never approach a lion if you see one.
- If you come upon a lion, face it. Stand upright and keep a large profile. If you are wearing a jacket, raise the back over your head to make you appear even bigger.
- Facing the lion, back away slowly if you can do so safely.
- If the lion acts aggressively, throw stones, branches, or whatever you can get your hands on without crouching down or turning your back.
- Wave your arms and speak firmly.
- Fight back if the lion attacks you. Remain standing or get back up if you are knocked down.

Bear Safety

- Most bears are easily frightened off, at least the smaller black bears found in the lower 48 states.
- Be extremely cautious around a sow and her cubs.
- If you see a bear, stop, stay calm, and back away slowly as you remain facing the bear.
- As you move away, talk loudly and let the bear discover your presence.
- Avoid direct eye contact, for bears may perceive this as a threat.
- Don't run away. You cannot out-run a bear, and they are likely to give chase.
- If attacked by a bear it is best to play dead and cover your neck and head with your arms and hands.

8

GETTING THERE

The road goes on forever,
but I can't without a rest.
It is high time for lunch.
    —*J.R.R. Tolkien (1892-1973)*

FROM THE LOGBOOK

   The trip that was supposed to take one and one half hours took almost six. The overcast sky, the snow was blowing in our faces, and the fact that we had missed the blue diamond was the beginning of a long, over-exerting trip. After realizing we weren't on the right track, we decided to turn back and hopefully find a blue diamond along the way.
   —**C.C., January 1995**

The adventure begins as soon as you load your vehicle and head for the trail. By then you've planned all of the details of your trip. Now it's time to put the plans to work. In this chapter, we cover tips for getting an early start, pacing, route-finding, and map-reading.

GET AN EARLY START

Designate a person to make wake-up calls to avoid the late-start syndrome. It's tough to get up early after a hard week at the office, but be brave and roll toward the coffeepot, not the down comforter. Or, get a hotel near the trailhead and have the front-desk people make the wake-up call for you. An early start will help keep you from stressing out should you encounter unexpected delays.

ADVANCE TRIP

It's possible to spend more time getting to and looking for the trail-head than traveling the actual trail. It helps to locate the trailhead well in advance of the trip. Go for a ski tour along your chosen trail to get familiar with the terrain. If you make it to the hut, consideration demands that you don't go in until your reservation date, but there is nothing wrong with checking out the trail to the cabin. A pre-trip check of the trailhead is also a good time to check out the neighboring town for coffee shops and for the hours of the local ski mountaineering shop for the inevitability that someone forget something.

DISCUSSIONS ON THE WAY

On the way to the trailhead, it's a good idea to discuss the weather, the route in, avalanche hazards and contingency plans. While chatting with your mates, you can find out if someone forgot something. Practice your mantras: "skis, boots, poles, hat, gloves, goggles," or "beer, bread, beacon, bacon, beans and Bordeaux."

CAR POOL AND CAR SHUTTLE

Many trailhead parking areas are small and have limited parking. Besides, carpooling is environmentally correct. If you will be doing a car shuttle for a point-to-point hut trip, allow plenty of extra time. You may need a high-clearance, four-wheel-drive vehicle to get to the trailhead.

A PERSONAL STORY

On our way to the trailhead, our low-clearance passenger vehicles were bottoming out on the ruts caused by wet spring conditions. We turned around and parked in a safe place (snow was expected while we were on our trip which would have made the road as slick as snot.) We all piled into Karen's truck and made it to the trailhead. Thankfully we had her truck, otherwise we would have had a six-mile walk just to get to the point where we could put on our skis and ski seven miles to the hut!

ON THE TRAIL

Many huts have more than one route in. You've picked the trail that works best for your group's ability, and you have a pretty good idea of how long the trip is going to take. It's a beautiful, blue-sky day and everybody is chomping at the bit. But wait a minute. There are a couple of things you should do first.

Check everyone's avalanche beacon to be sure it works. This only takes a few seconds. Have one person travel up the trail one hundred feet

Check signs at the trailhead for important information before heading out.
Photo by Leigh Girvin Yule

or so and turn his or her beacon to receive. That person listens to everyone else's beacon as they move by. Make sure someone checks the tester's beacon as well.

Discuss the weather and how it might change. When you made your reservation months or even a year in advance, you couldn't know what the weather would be doing by the time your trip rolled around. Be prepared for bright sunlight and the blizzard of the century. If the weather is worsening, avalanche conditions may be changing and route-finding may become more difficult. Look for changing snow conditions and potential avalanche indicators, such as the wind blowing snow off peaks and ridges, collapsing or *whumphing* sounds as you ski or snowshoe along.

Pull out your map and compass to get oriented and started in the right direction. Once on the trail, check in with each other. The group leader should check on all members of the group periodically to see how things are going and ask, "Are we all happy campers?" If a group member checked out the trail before the trip, be sure to ask him or her if everyone is heading in the right direction.

If you see something interesting while on the trail, point it out to other members of the group. You may see unusual animal tracks, such as lynx or marten, or the wing marks from a bird taking off from the snow—maybe it was a hawk that just caught lunch.

Getting to the hut is a large part of the hut experience, but if you focus on the destination, you risk missing the good things along the way—the sights, sounds, and smells of the trail. Plan your trip so you have time to enjoy it all.

TIPS FROM THE PROS

The larger the group, the greater the "fiddle factor."
For each additional person, your travel time increases 5 to 10
percent. When in a large group, it often becomes a party, and no
one is keeping tabs on each other. Large groups should consider
a buddy system.
— Scott Messina, Aspen Alpine Guides.

TIPS FROM EXPERIENCED HUT-TRIPPERS

As a rule of thumb, backcountry skiers travel at about one mile per hour. Add one hour for each one thousand feet of elevation gain.

PACE YOURSELVES

Once on the trail, you may begin to feel as if the trail goes on forever, and you'll never reach the hut. Settle into your own pace. Don't let a speedier skier dictate your speed. It could put a damper on the rest of your trip. If you tour the backcountry enough, you will find a pace that works best for you.

If you're traveling in a large party, expect people to split up into smaller groups. Always travel in pairs and let each other know how you're feeling. Faster travelers should stop at all trail junctions or confusing sections in the trail in order to maintain contact with the slower trekkers. Don't rely on writing messages in the snow. The rest of your party may be practicing the art of Zen pacing and go right by your well-worded note.

The group leader plays a very important role in setting the pace, and making sure that those who know the trail wait and check up on the slower travelers.

Some people will tell you that the experience on the trail reaches near mystical proportions. Others who haven't packed well or are not in shape will swear-off any future trips. One story from a hut log describes a party of birthday revelers traveling with especially heavy packs. They started late and had taken the steepest trail. In order to reach the hut before dark, two people had to haul two packs at a time up the trail for the rest of the group.

TRAIL MARKINGS

Blue diamonds are a common trail marker for cross-country ski trails. In wilderness areas, you might see a series of blazes, squares of bark removed with a hatchet from a tree. Above treeline you should look for cairns, piles of stones marking the trail. Some hut systems have no trail markings at all, and you'll have to rely on your map and compass. Whatever the case, don't depend on trail markings. Trees blow down, vandals remove diamonds and signs, and deep snow may cover cairns and blue diamonds.

FINDING THE ROUTE

Some people have an innate sense of direction and can find north as though they had a magnet in their head. Others get hopelessly lost. It's helpful to know if your companion is a good map reader before you rely on him or her to find the way to the hut. Good backcountry travelers regularly look over their shoulders to find landmarks for the return journey—maybe the trail jogs left at the old, gnarled tree, or the spired ridge is close

Blue diamonds are commonly used to mark cross-country ski trails.
Photo by Pete Wingle

FROM THE LOGBOOK

We had trouble finding the hut. The last mile was not well marked. A real problem with new snow and no tracks to follow.

to the main trail. Watch good route-finders, and you will see this over-the-shoulder-navigating in action.

A map and compass are required tools for route-finding. Altimeters are also valuable for knowing elevation and pinpointing your location on the map. Altimeters, however, need constant calibration. Recalibrate your altimeter any time you get to a known elevation such as a pass, a stream confluence, trailhead, or lake.

Route-finding requires skill. Use every backcountry trip as a route-finding exercise, even if you know where you are. Then, if the time ever comes when you really need the skills, you'll have them.

USE YOUR MAP AND COMPASS

Using a map and compass is called navigating or orienteering. Proper use of a map and compass lets you know where you are, and the location of the cabin in relation to your position. Refer regularly to your map and compass throughout your trip. If you don't use them, by the time you need

Tools for navigation include map, compass, altimeter, scale, and GPS unit.
Photo by Pete Wingle

them it's too late. If you don't know where you are, you can't know where you are going.

Maps with routes to the cabins are generally available from the reservations department. But many people don't bring a map because they think the route is well-marked or because they don't know how to read one. A common problem for the directionally impaired is to position the map with its north end facing north. If in doubt, use your compass to find north.

On topographic maps, the parallel squiggly lines are contour lines. They indicate terrain and elevation; the closer together the lines, the steeper the terrain. The farther apart the lines, the gentler the terrain. Heavier weight brown lines will be marked with the elevation. The map legend will tell you what the distance is between contour lines and may also tell you what various symbols mean. On some maps green areas will indicate forest and white areas indicate open meadows or areas above timberline. The scale of the map let's you know the size of the area as well as the distance you have to travel to get where you want to go.

Use landmarks on the map that correspond with features you see on the ground—a river crossing, odd-shaped spires and knobs, timberline, and nearby peaks—to help you locate where you are. Use your knowledge of aspects (the direction the slope faces) and your knowledge of vegetation to help you get oriented. North-aspect slopes usually have deeper, softer snow than south-aspect slopes. Vegetation is sparse on the drier south-aspect slopes, and terrain features are generally less steep as glaciation had less of an impact there. East-facing slopes have early morning sunlight and west-aspects have late afternoon sun.

Study the map carefully before your tour begins. Know the terrain before you get there by building an image of the topography in your mind. In this way you prepare yourself for critical junctions and navigation be easier.

Excellent books on using maps and compasses are readily available, and many outdoor-equipment stores and outing clubs offer clinics as well. Using a map and compass in a controlled environment, like a class or your living room, makes it easier to understand compass bearings and other route-finding techniques. Success with a map and compass in a blizzard above treeline requires not only knowledge and skill but a lot of practice.

TIPS FROM EXPERIENCED HUT-TRIPPERS

In a white-out, navigate by sending someone ahead a short distance, then use them as a compass bearing. In this manner, leap-frog across the terrain. It's tedious but effective.

At least a couple of people in your group should be experienced with maps and compasses in order to check each other. When someone is cold, tired, and hungry, it's easy to make mistakes. Don't ever place the welfare of the entire group upon the shoulders of just one person.

In addition to using maps and compasses, consider getting a guidebook. Several books with detailed instructions on how to get to the huts are now available. See the bibliography for more information on these books.

GLOBAL POSITIONING SYSTEMS

A nifty little gadget called the global positioning system (GPS) is expensive, but may be worth the money. It tells you how far you are from a pre-programmed destination and directs you how to get there. In order to be accurate and to tell you the exact latitude and longitude of your destination, the GPS unit must have access to three geostationary satellites in space. One drawback of the GPS unit is that it directs you to your destination in a straight line. It's up to you to figure out how to get around that cliff or across the raging river. A few huts and yurts have plotted GPS locations. Ask your reservationist if GPS locations are available for the hut you've chosen.

A PERSONAL STORY

Our story is one about too much preparation and too little actual knowledge. . .another way of putting it—the pathway to failure is often paved with good intentions.

We were going to make "the trip" with friends who were familiar with the rigors and requirements of mountain travel and cross-country skiing. We even planned to make a "recon" of the area prior to our ascent. We never made the recon, however, and at the last minute the other couple had to pull out. I had limited experience in cross-country skiing and my wife thought she was quite the jock. With this "boost" of confidence, we decided to make the trip alone.

We had packed everything. My pack weighed roughly 50 pounds, my wife Sandy's approximately 20 pounds. Our packs burst with everything from MRE's (Meals Ready to Eat), sleeping bags, snowshoes, entrenching tools (that's a shovel), extra clothes, half shelter, extra clothes, water, extra clothes, compass, knives, and extra clothes. . . .Sandy "packed" our packs.

The initial part of the trail was very steep (not really) and tiring (really). After about a mile (really 1/4 mile) we decided it would be much easier to use our snowshoes. So we buried our skis and proceeded. Never mind that neither of us had ever done any serious snowshoeing or that our "government issue" showshoes (you know, the kind made from wood and cat gut) were wider than the newer, lighter models, and were, in fact, too wide for the trail. Did I mention that they kept coming off and we kept falling down and the packs kept getting heavier and heavier?

As we approached the last leg of "the trip," we encountered some folks who had been at the cabin the previous night. "How much farther?" I asked. "Not too far, about a mile, but it's all uphill, real steep," they responded. Uphill?! What the heck have we been doing for the last 5 hours (yes, it was almost 2:00 pm). I looked at the map and sure enough the contour lines merged into one big, black mass, revealing a serious and long ascent. We chose to retrace our steps and head back.

The moral of our story: do some serious cross-country skiing prior to attempting a trip. (We didn't even have skins for our skis!) If you're a novice, go with someone experienced. The mountains are as unforgiving of fools as they are beautiful to those people who are prepared to enjoy them.

— *Buzz Geiger, Major, U.S. Army*

As mentioned earlier, never rely on blue diamonds or someone else's ski tracks to get you where you're going. On our first hut trip, we followed a ski track to an open meadow where that trail turned into dozens of ski tracks with no indication as to which, if any, led to the hut. Only with the proper use of a map and compass was our party able to locate the hut.

Some groups never find their hut and are forced to backtrack to their vehicles, cold, wet and disenchanted with the backcountry experience. What to do in these circumstances will be discussed in Chapter 9, Not Getting There.

9

NOT GETTING THERE

There are other Annapurnas in the lives of men.

—Maurice Herzog (1919-)

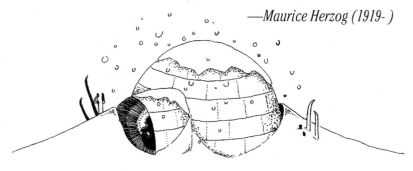

At 11:30 P.M., David Schweppe was at the 10th Mountain Division Hut doing routine maintenance when a man stumbled into the cabin, hypothermic, dehydrated, and disoriented, begging for help. His friends were a mile back on the trail.

After a few minutes by the stove and something hot to drink, the man became coherent and was able to lead Schweppe to his three companions. They found them shivering in sleeping bags, their frozen boots piled in the snow nearby. With much struggle and difficulty, Schweppe was able to get boots on two of them, but one of the women could not get her frozen feet into her frozen boots. Schweppe duct-taped her feet, clad only in wool socks, to the back of his skis. Slowly, he shuffled with her to the cabin.

The group had been at Uncle Bud's Hut the night before, had spent the morning skiing, and didn't depart for the 10th Mountain Division Hut, over seven miles away, until one in the afternoon. At 4:30 P.M. a storm hit. At 10:30 P.M., they realized they couldn't find the hut, and that they weren't prepared to spend the night outside. Three hunkered down while the strongest member of the group went in search of the cabin.

What lessons can be learned from this experience? Get to your destination, then spend your free time skiing. Always be prepared to spend the night outside.

According to the hut reservations staff, the top five reasons for not reaching a hut are: getting too late a start from the trailhead, overestimating your ability level or that of your group, poor route-finding skills, failure to ski together, and inadequate planning.

LATE STARTS

In Chapter 8, Getting There, we discussed the importance of getting an early start. Ideally, you'll want to get to the cabin around one or two in the afternoon so you have time to solve problems should they arise on the way, or time to ski, or play if things go smoothly.

December and January have short daylight hours. You might be able to travel at night under a full moon, but with no moon, or in blizzard conditions, night navigation is difficult at best. If you suspect you'll be on the trail late, carry headlamps and other handy gear such as a spare pair of dry mittens, a stove and melting pot, and clear-lensed glasses or goggles easily accessible either near the top of your pack or in your parka pocket.

OVER-ESTIMATING ABILITY LEVEL

If you're familiar with your group and have shared numerous trips, you'll know each other's abilities and can judge how long it will take you to get to the hut. If yours is a first-time hut trip, be conservative. Plan a trip to a hut which is an easy distance from the trailhead to gain an appreciation of the skills required for a longer adventure.

Blisters, inclement weather, or equipment failures can conspire against you and slow you down. Short pre-tour trips into the backcountry as a group will help iron out equipment glitches, give you a chance to rehearse blister treatments, and if the weather is poor, help you learn to deal with inclement weather.

POOR ROUTE-FINDING

One common reason for not reaching your destination is a result of poor route-finding skills, especially in bad weather when conditions deteriorate quickly and unexpectedly. The trail may become hidden by falling snow, and you may find yourself in white-out conditions.

FAILING TO STAY TOGETHER

A recent hut near-disaster was an incident near Aspen in February 1993. A group of seven with varying levels of experience traveled into the

Alfred Braun Hut system during one of the worst blizzard cycles of the winter. It wasn't long before they had split into three parties, each struggling to survive. Through luck they all lived, but many suffered frostbite and haven't spoken to each other since.

Every changing situation in the backcountry requires decisions and accommodations. In most circumstances it's best to keep the group together. The combined skills of the group and access to everyone's gear will help you stay warm, calm, and alive.

INADEQUATE PLANNING

Inadequate planning becomes evident when you have to bivouac along the trail. What kind of food are you carrying? A five-pound, uncooked pot roast isn't worth much if your party is stranded overnight. Did you underestimate the time required to arrive at your destination? Early starts give you the grace period necessary to reach the hut before dark.

During group meetings did you plan for the possibility of having to survive a night outdoors? Did you bring the necessary gear? Appendix E includes a list of gear necessary to spend a comfortable night out. Check it out and make copies for all group members.

Sometimes all the planning and preparedness in the world doesn't help when Mother Nature throws roadblocks in the way. Winter storms can create conditions requiring trail-breaking through deep snow. Mike Zobbe, a hut master for Summit Huts Association, participated in the 10th Mountain Interconnect, a hut traverse from Aspen to Vail. The trip started during one of Colorado's heaviest storm cycles in January of 1996. He recalls that the group had to contend with a minimum of two and a half feet of new snow on the trail every day for a solid week, slowing the group to a half mile per hour. If heavy snow is in the forecast, you may have to plan on long and tiring days on the trail.

IF YOU WANT TO TURN BACK

Don't let the fact that you're lost take the fun out of not knowing where you are. You have two choices when it becomes apparent that you won't make it to the hut—turn back, or plan on an overnight bivouac. Never be afraid to turn back. The huts are not going anywhere, and you can always visit another time. It's difficult to go on another hut trip if you're dead.

What do you do if half the group wants to press on and half the group

Be sure to get your bearings with topographic features whenever visibility allows.
Photo by Scott Toepfer

wants to turn back to the car? Risking friendship over losing the small cost of a hut reservation is not worth it. Whatever you decide, try to stay together. It's always the best insurance policy for surviving a night outdoors.

If you turn back, make sure everyone is stocked with full water bottles, food, and dry clothes. Stay together. Remember, it's much easier to become separated in the dark than during daylight. If you need to break out the stove and melt snow for water and have a bite to eat, do it. Get fueled up for the return journey—it will likely be difficult.

EMERGENCY SHELTERS

If you're unable to make it back to the car, you'll have to spend the night outdoors. Your survival kit should contain a bivy sac, Space Blanket or tent, thermal pad, shovel, camp stove and pot, and food for a comfortable night out. You can build several types of emergency shelters for protection. If you're prepared, a night outdoors can be a magnificent adventure instead of a frightful struggle to stay alive.

Snow caves don't have to be cold, gloomy, wet, or oppressive. On the contrary, they can be lovely places to spend the night. But building a good snow cave takes about an hour. As soon as you've decided to stay out, get started. The exercise you'll get while you build a good cave will help keep

Foul weather makes for poor visibility, and it can be difficult to find the route.
Photo by John Warner

you warm. If you get cold in the night, redecorate.

A common problem for cave builders is to have the snow cave collapse. Finding the right snow is essential. You need dense snow. If you can cut blocks out of the snow with your shovel it will be dense enough to dig a cave. It's possible to dig a snow cave without a shovel, but it's a cold and wet undertaking.

You'll need to find a snowdrift a minimum of six feet deep. Do not dig your snow cave in avalanche terrain. Begin digging at the low end of the drift and dig about three feet in. Then cut a vertical shaft upward where the main room will be. The living area should be enough above the entrance so that warm air will be trapped there. Excavate an area large

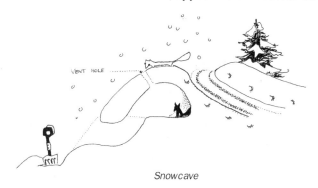

Snowcave

enough for comfort; take care to make the roof concave so that melting snow will run down the walls and not onto your head. Don't forget to dig a vent through the roof for fresh air. You can make this vent hole bigger if the cave becomes too warm. Once the cave is finished, spread out a tarp, thermal pad, or bivy sac on the floor. Keep track of your equipment, which could melt into the snow and be lost until spring.

Another type of emergency winter shelter is a snow trench. Dig a stepped trench into the snow for sleeping platforms and carve blocks which can form a slanted roof over the trench. This shelter will also require dense, compacted snow in order to keep the roof from collapsing.

Finally, if you can't find a suitable snowdrift you may be able to find a heavily-branched tree around which you can build an igloo, or use for a makeshift lean-to.

Snow shelters do not need to be complex affairs. Survival is the key. The next time you're out for a day tour, build a snow cave for fun and practice. Practice your survival techniques before an emergency arises.

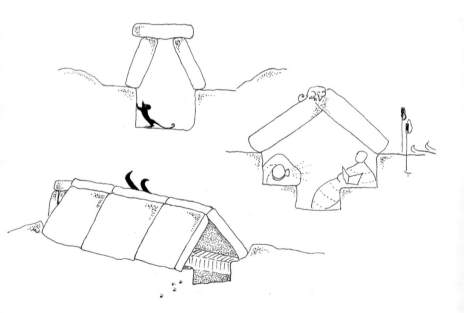

Snow trench

Snow, Snow Everywhere and Not a Drop. . .

If you're caught out in the open for the night, one of the greatest hazards you'll face is dehydration. Your body loses enormous amounts of water with the day's exertion, and you'll need to replenish these lost fluids. You should drink two quarts of water each day when backcountry skiing. "Drink little but drink often," is an old saying that still holds true.

There are few sources of flowing water in winter, so you need at least one stove for melting snow. While some people are building the emergency shelter, others can be melting snow for cooking and drinking. Once you're settled into the shelter, keep the water from freezing. It's very discouraging to wake up in the morning to a frozen water bottle. If necessary, keep your water bottle warm by keeping it next to you in your sleeping bag.

Dehydration contributes to hypothermia, winter's greatest killer. Hypothermia occurs when your body temperature drops dangerously below normal. If you see any signs of hypothermia in someone, such as uncontrolled shivering or disoriented actions, quickly replace his or her wet clothing with dry clothing. For more on hypothermia and other first-aid related topics see Chapter 15, First Aid and Rescue.

Your body needs fuel as well as water. Athletes have developed a term for running out of fuel during competition. They call it "bonk," referring to complete physical and mental inability to continue. Carry enough easily-eaten food to keep your engine fueled.

When To Go For Help

Eventually the question will arise as to whether you should go for help. This is the time when an experienced, calm, and knowledgeable group leader is worth more than his or her weight in gold. Cool heads need to prevail because search and rescue teams will take hours to respond to any report of an accident in the backcountry. Search and rescue teams won't risk their lives to save yours. A good group leader will be necessary to keep potentially dangerous situations from deteriorating into chaos. Remember, before you set out on a hut trip, you should have the tools and the means to deal with almost any situation. You should be able to make a sled from an injured person's skis and to make splints for arms and legs. Self-reliance takes practice.

Becoming comfortable in the winter outdoors takes time and experience. Go out on full-moon trips to become comfortable with the night, spend long days in bitter-cold temperatures to learn what you need to stay warm, practice making snow shelters, and take avalanche and first-aid courses. These are the only ways to gain the experience you must have when traveling in the backcountry.

OUR MOST UNUSUAL HUT TRIP

It was a beautiful January day. We'd heard Vance's Cabin was easy to get to, so we took our time and got off about noon. The snow was fantastic on Tennessee Pass, so we dropped our packs and made a few runs before getting serious about finding the trail again. There was some discussion at the intersection whether we should go north or south, but we finally decided it had to be north based on our topo map.

Off we went, humming a happy tune until we had skied for awhile and still no hut. Out came the map and more discussion, but we decided the cabin must be around the corner. Down, down we skied until suddenly it was 4:30 P.M. Night comes early in January. We knew we had screwed up. Luckily there were only the two of us—no other unlucky friends were depending on us to find the hut.

I was tired, and it was dark, so innocently I asked, "What would the Boy Scouts do?" Instantly Charlie said, "Camp!" We didn't have much equipment for camping other than our two sleeping bags and one space blanket. Luckily we had an Outside Magazine to tear up and start a fire. The fire cheered me but it was January and colder than the proverbial well-digger's backside.

I put little spots of insulation (gaiters, headband) whereever I had body contact with the snow. I nestled against my water bottle to keep it from freezing. Sleep doesn't come easily when you're shivering like crazy. I don't think I slept all night.

Finally, as if a gift from on high, the pitch dark became gray. I rejoiced, feeling grateful to be alive, and a little chickadee joined in. . . life was looking up.
— Jan Prowell, Frisco

AT THE HUT

*There was the fire, snapping
and crackling and promising life
with every dancing flame.*
—*Jack London (1876-1916)*

You've traveled miles through the backcountry, and now you arrive at the hut. Your heart beats a little faster, not from exertion, but from the excitement and relief of finally getting there.

If other guests are already at the cabin, say hello and introduce yourself. You have something special in common—a love of the backcountry. If you're the first guests to arrive at the hut, light a fire and gather and start melting snow for water. Shovel the decks and a path to the outhouse (before you take your boots off!). Post your hut confirmation letter, read the hut instructions, find and organize your sleeping space, and relax. You've arrived! Congratulate yourselves.

Soon after arriving at the hut, you'll want a place to put your pack and possessions. Consolidate your possessions and your group. Find beds or bunks and keep your stuff there. Some things to look for when choosing your space are: privacy (You may be lucky enough to get one of the few private bedrooms at the hut.), windows, nearby hooks and shelves, and proximity to your companions.

One of the pleasures of the huts is living with fire—splitting the kindling, building the fire, tending it, and stirring the coals. The crackle and pop of burning logs, the solid thwack of ax on wood, the fire's warm radiance and mesmerizing flame, and the smell of wood smoke are comforts in cold weather. In this modern age of wood-burning restrictions and gas fireplaces, many people don't live with a wood fire as a heat source and don't realize what a lot of work it is to keep it going. It will take the group's concerted effort to split and stock the wood, maintain the fire, and keep the cabin warm. But the work is always rewarded by the pleasure of the warmth and the bright, dancing flame.

BUILDING A FIRE

Look for and read any instructions posted near the stove for proper operation. Remove excess ashes from the woodstove. (See below for instructions on how to dispose of them.) Leave some ashes in the stove; they make a nice bed for embers. Place all materials for the fire near the woodstove: newspaper (or other fire starter), small pieces of wood (kindling), medium pieces of wood, large pieces of wood, and matches or lighter.

Be sure the dampers and flue are open for good airflow. The instructions should tell you the correct position. Crumple up four to six sheets of newspaper and put them in a tight pile in the center of the firebox. Place the kindling in the shape of a teepee over the newspaper and light it. Close the door on the woodstove partway, leaving it open just a crack for maximum airflow.

Woodstoves are the center of activity inside huts and are used for melting snow, drying clothes, and warming cold, tired bodies. Photo by Brian Litz

As the kindling catches fire, and the fire grows, add medium-size pieces of wood. Then add the larger pieces of wood as the fire grows. Make sure the fire has air to breathe. Once the fire is established, close the door and dampers to slow the rate of burn and to conserve fuel. In well-insulated huts, let the fire burn down before bedtime; in yurts, you'll want to stoke the fire.

Split firewood and kindling on the large splitting stumps in the wood room. Don't split wood on the brick or stone hearths because they can break.

For tips on how to light a fire in a wood-burning cookstove, see Chapter 12, In the Kitchen.

Avoiding Problems

Be sure the flue and dampers are open. Lack of air will smother a fire. Don't put large pieces of wood on the fire too soon. They won't catch and may also smother the flame. If this happens, remove the large pieces of wood (use tongs or fireproof gloves) and start over. Place the charred logs in the ash bucket until the fire is hot enough to burn them.

Some older stoves with folding doors are temperamental and need a good draft to get going. A draft is created by drawing air up the vent, usually located at the base of the firebox in a rear corner. To facilitate this draft, be sure to remove all of the ashes from the firebox. You may need to arrange your kindling into a stacked platform to provide adequate airflow.

Take precautions. Keep doors to the wood stove closed except when starting or stoking the fire to prevent embers from popping out and starting a blaze. Don't try to burn plastic, foil, aluminum cans, coated paper such as magazine stock, or other toxic materials. Be careful not to hang polypropylene or other synthetic materials too close to the stove. These materials can melt.

Dealing with Ashes and Hot Coals

The hut should be equipped with a metal coal scuttle or metal ash can. If you need to remove ashes and coals before building a fire, use the metal shovel designed specifically for this purpose and place the ashes in the metal container. When the ash container is full, transfer the ashes to the larger, metal ash cans, usually found on a back deck, under a deck, or near the rear entry. *Never* put ashes or coals in a paper bag or other flammable container. Even if you think they're cool, they may contain a live ember. Many condominiums in ski country have burned down because guests used this careless method when disposing of ashes.

FIREWOOD

Firewood is stocked at the huts in fall. Some hut systems cut and split the wood for you. Others provide only sawed rounds which you have to split yourself. Stocking firewood is one of the most expensive and time-consuming chores in outfitting a hut. Many volunteer hours are required to move, cut, split, and stack the firewood, so please conserve it by burning only what you need.

To make kindling, find a piece of wood that you can balance on its flat end. It should be relatively free of knots and branches in order to spilt it easily. Never hold the piece of wood while you attempt to chop it. If you do, your fingers may end up in the kindling pile.

Some people like to wear glasses or goggles when splitting wood to protect their eyes from flying splinters. Keep children out of the wood room at all times. This protects them from the dangers of splinters, axes, and heavy logs. While you're chopping kindling, make enough to start a fire that day and the next morning. As a courtesy, always leave extra kindling for the next guests.

OUTDOOR FIRE PITS

Some huts provide an outdoor fire pit for summer campfires; others don't because some wild animals are attracted to the smell of food being cooked outside. Furthermore, an outdoor fire left unattended, even for a moment, can start a devastating wildfire.

WET CLOTHES

Space around the stoves for drying is at a premium. Use it for critical garments such as socks, hats, gloves, and boot-liners. Hang outerwear on hooks in the boot room or some other out-of-the-way place. Once your clothes are dry, put them away so that others may use the limited drying space around the stove.

TOILETS

Most huts have either an outdoor pit toilet or an indoor composting toilet. A notable exception is the Shrine Mountain Inn in Colorado which has running water, flush toilets, and showers. Colorado's San Juan Huts are also memorable for a toilet seat positioned over a trash can. Some toilets don't even have a house, giving new meaning to the word outhouse.

Most pit toilets are located some distance from the hut. You'll need to venture out into the cold, so keep your boots handy. Other huts have outhouses connected to them by a short wooden walkway. Most huts have a one-seater. A "toilet flag," usually a blue trail diamond, hangs near the door. Take it with you when you go to the restroom so that others know the toilet is occupied and be sure to put it back when you're finished.

Outdoor Pit Toilets

A pit toilet is a lined vault in the ground that contains human waste until a pumper truck can pump it out in summer. If the toilet has been designed to U.S. Forest Service standards for a S.S.T. (Sweet Smelling Toilet), it will be remarkably odor-free and pleasant to use. Many pit toilets at huts don't meet these standards, however, and are quite stinky, especially in the spring when things start to thaw.

Don't put trash, tampons, sanitary napkins, food, or anything other than human waste in pit toilets. These items clog pumper-truck lines.

Trash-Can Toilets

Be sure to take the lid off the trash can before using this toilet or you'll have a mess to clean up. When full, trash cans are sealed and driven or flown out in the summer to a local sewage treatment plant.

A rustic outdoor toilet. Photo by Paul Sommer

Composting Toilets

The Summit Huts in Colorado have indoor composting toilets, a happy step up from outdoor pit toilets. Sawdust, added to the composter after each use, acts as a bulking and aerating medium. Vent fans, powered by solar energy, draw odor and moisture out and away. Active bacteria break down the human waste, decomposing it into a humus-like material that is spread away from the cabin and trail in the forest in fall.

As with pit toilets, only human waste and toilet paper go in the composter. Trash, tampons, sanitary napkins, and food interfere with the composting process and have to be picked out by hand.

There is a potential drawback to composting toilets. If the photovoltaic system is drained, the fan won't work and the toilets get smelly fast. That should be an incentive to use electric lights sparingly and to keep the photovoltaic system charged!

PHOTOVOLTAICS (SOLAR POWER)

Most huts are equipped with 12- or 24-volt DC solar-powered lights, which make it easier and more pleasant to prepare meals, play games, or read, than it is under the narrow beam of a headlamp. Always remember to bring your headlamp or flashlight to the huts, however, for the solar system is not fail-proof. Extended periods of cloudy days or heavy use drain the batteries, and a day or more of sunshine is required to recharge them.

A hut trip is the first time many guests will use photovoltaic (PV) power. Log books are filled with comments about how impressed guests are with PV efficiency, reliability, simplicity, and environmental friendliness. Photovoltaics provide electricity for lights, vent fans, and, in some cases, fire-alarm systems, but you won't find plugs for your blow dryer or blender.

When you arrive at a hut or at dusk, turn on the circuit breakers found at the load center, which looks something like the circuit-breaker box in your home. Be sure to turn off the circuit breakers in the morning or upon departure so that you won't inadvertently drain the system.

Many load centers have a series of gauges that tell you how much energy is left in the batteries. Keep an eye on these gauges. If the batteries start to run down (sometimes indicated by a yellow warning light), use electric lights sparingly to conserve energy.

How Solar Power Works

Photovoltaics convert sunlight to electricity. Sunlight hits solar electric panels (or modules) mounted on the exterior of a cabin or on a distant pole and it is converted to electricity through a chemical process.

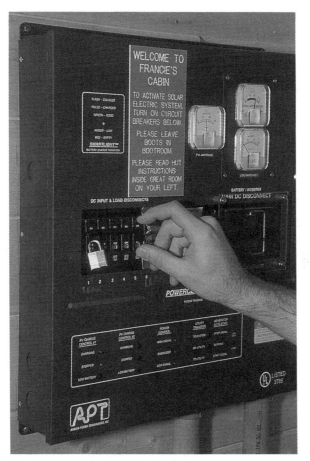

A typical load center box for a photovoltaic system.
Photo by Todd Powell

Electric power is stored in deep-cycle, rechargeable batteries, similar to golf-cart batteries. While the power of the sun is unlimited, the storage capacity of the batteries is not.

ALTERNATIVE LIGHT SOURCES

Most huts are equipped with alternative light sources should the photovoltaic system not work. Most commonly, you will find propane-fueled lanterns and extra propane canisters or flashlights. Kerosene lanterns are rare because of the potential for fire. Some hut systems provide candles, others do not because of the fire hazard. Propane canisters and batteries are not recyclable and are costly to provide, so please use alternative lights sparingly.

COMMUNICATIONS

Communication from or into the huts is usually not possible. Some huts have radios for the hut master to use in emergencies, but they frequently don't work. The Appalachian Mountain Club's huts have radios for emergency use and to receive weather updates each morning.

BEFORE YOU GO TO BED

Split firewood so you have kindling to start a fire in the morning.

Close the dampers to let the fire burn down (when in yurts, stoke the fire).

Fill snow buckets and the snowmelt pot on the stove, so you have plenty of water in the morning.

If you have to get an early start, organize breakfast foods, clean the hut, get your things organized, and pack up as much as you can.

RULES AND REGULATIONS

There are many rules and regulations regarding use of huts. Some typical regulations you'll find at most huts are: no dogs, no use without a valid reservation (i.e. no poaching), no motor vehicles, no fireworks, no smoking. For more information, see Appendix A, Rules and Policies

THE HUT SYSTEM MANAGER'S RESPONSIBILITIES

The hut system manager occasionally sends a hut keeper to make sure a cabin hasn't burned down and that it is being well-taken care of. The hut keeper will clean toilets or maintain the composter, re-stock supplies such as toilet paper, paper towels, and dish soap, and check fire alarms and extinguishers. The hut keeper is not responsible for hauling out trash or for general cleaning. If you notice something that needs maintenance, contact the hut manager as soon as you return to civilization.

The airy, well-lit interior of the Hidden Treasure Yurt, near Edwards, Colorado. Photo by Terri Thomas

PLAY AND PRACTICE

Once you've figured out how the hut works, get down to some serious play. Practice your telemark turn—feel the wind on your cheeks and the bend in your knees. For the many cross-country skiers who haven't mastered the telemark turn, the following brief lesson by Paul Parker should help.

THE TELEMARK STANCE

by Paul Parker
(Adapted from Free-Heel Skiing; second edition)

The telemark's semi-kneeling, genuflecting position has superior fore-to-aft stability. It braces the skier to help prevent uncomfortable forward falls. There are a number of ways to learn the telemark turn. Below we will outline two of our favorites. First, the telemark stance:

The Telemark Stance

Your body position is fundamental. Start on a flat spot with the telemark stance, using an athletic body position: a round, relaxed back, stomach pulled in, then sink straight down, sliding one foot forward and one foot back. Your weight should stay evenly distributed between both feet. Experiment with a very tall stance, and find a comfortable spot in the middle. You should feel your weight resting on your whole front foot and on the ball of your rear foot.

Learning the Tele from a Striding Position

In the flats, stride from one telemark position to another. Take exaggerated, bent-legged strides. Move as though you're trying to stay low and invisible in tall grass. It should be as much a sense of dropping down as it is striding forward.

You'll need a good practice slope. Pick a very gentle packed downhill that you can run without fear. Point your skis straight down the slope, push off, and make these same striding moves down the hill. Terrain selection is important for this exercise; you need a slow downhill slope that allows you to run straight with your skis flat.

Now you're ready to try a telemark turn. At the same time that you stride into a new telemark position, steer (twist) your front foot into a turn. Remember that the foot you're pointing with is the outside foot, and you're pointing it to the inside of the turn. Try turns one at a time, on each side. Turn your skis across the hill until you come to a stop. As you progress, think not only of your foot, but point your ski, foot, and knee into the turn.

As you gain confidence, while still on your easiest slope, start striding from turn to turn. Make your turns smaller, using the striding motion mentioned above, steering each forward foot, ski, and knee inside the turn. Once you get your balance, you'll find yourself striding from little tele to little tele and making S curves.

An experienced skier makes the stable and elegant telemark turn. Photo by Scott Toepfer

When you go out to explore, take the opportunity to evaluate the snowpack for avalanche potential and to further your avalanche awareness. When skiing, practice resource conservation. In Utah the combination of many skiers and limited areas for backcountry skiing requires skiing close to your partners tracks by spooning or doing figure 8s to leave more of that valuable resource, untracked powder, for the next skier.

After new snow has turned to the consistency of old, white glue, enterprising hut trippers find other things to do. Many cabins have begun to accumulate an inventory of saucers and sleds. Music and the arts are represented at the huts by well-stocked libraries, guitars, harmonicas, spoons, photographs, and drawings in the hut log books.

Sometimes a hut system will offer special-event trips: clinics in photography, cooking, yoga, avalanche beacon use, painting, writing workshops, and slide shows to name a few. One of the special events that fills up quickly are the full-moon tours. A full moon above timberline is a spectacle that needs to be experienced to be believed.

Games are popular for passing evening hours. Most huts have a few popular board games, or you can make your own fun with the classics like truth or dare, spin the bottle, or charades.

SAUNAS

Many of the larger huts in Colorado have saunas. For the Finns, the masters of the modern sauna, it was a kind of altar, an understandable connection in a county cloaked in darkness and cold much of the year. The sauna is an intense spiritual and physical experience; it warms both the body and the soul.

A proper sauna takes time. Sauna aficionados claim that three warm-up and cool-down sessions make for the ideal sauna experience. You'll need a minimum of an hour to heat up the sauna and another hour to an hour and a half to enjoy it.

Many sauna stoves are temperamental and take time to light. Lots of paper and small pieces of wood should help get the fire going in the firebox. Plan to spend some time near the sauna after you've lit the fire, and then time to stoke it.

Some people prefer a dry sauna so that their body can break into a sweat on its own. Others prefer to help the body along by throwing water or snow on the sauna stove. Be careful to add the snow or water gradually, or you'll feel like you've been hit by an atomic blast.

An immediate change in your body temperature is one of the joys of the sauna. When you've had enough heat, go outside and roll in the snow, or drench yourself with cold water.

Keep the snow outside the sauna clean. No trash, ashes, or yellow snow near the sauna. Don't take showers, use soap, or wash your hair in the sauna. The sauna building can't handle the extra moisture created when people use large amounts of water to rinse off inside. Soaps and shampoos make the floor slimy and are impossible to clean up. Don't smoke or burn candles in the sauna.

The Finnish code of sauna conduct asks that you refrain from loud talking, swearing, boasting, noisemaking, singing, and clapping in the sauna. Be an adult. The sauna is not a sexual experience. For more on the sauna and your health, see Chapter 14, To Your Health.

TIPS FROM EXPERIENCED HUT-TRIPPERS

When leaving the hut for a day of skiing, hiking, or exploring, remember to lock the cabin to protect it and your possessions from unwanted visitors.

Boot liners make good hut slippers in a pinch. But don't rely on them as your only hut slipper. Boot liners damage easily and can be expensive or impossible to replace.

PROBLEMS AT THE HUT

Problem. . . a perplexing question, situation or person.
—Webster's New Collegiate Dictionary, *2nd edition, 1956*

On occasion, things go wrong at the huts. The solar power may be drained, or the toilet may not be clean. You can resolve some of the problems by yourself, others will require a visit by the hut keeper.

FIRE

Fire is a real danger at the huts, so guests must be especially careful with wood-burning stoves, candles, and cooktops. *Never* use backpacking camp stoves inside huts.

The huts are equipped with smoke detectors and fire extinguishers. Note where the extinguishers are located in case you need to grab one quickly.

Familiarize yourself with all hut exits. Plan the escape route you would use in a fire emergency. An escape from an upper level may require using a rope ladder which should be in a box on the floor under the window.

If a fire starts and gets out of uncontrol, evacuate everybody immediately—with boots, clothing, and as much survival gear, as possible.

PROPANE LEAKS

Propane gas is highly flammable and toxic when breathed in high concentrations. If you smell a propane leak at the hut, and the odor is not too strong, attempt to locate the source of the leak. It may be a propane burner left on by accident, or perhaps the pilot light in a propane heating unit has gone out. Do not create any spark or flame. Don't even turn on the circuit breakers at the load center for the photovoltaic system as they may create enough spark to cause a propane explosion.

Open windows and doors to air out the building. Propane gas is heavier than air and will sink, so open doors and windows on the main or lower level first.

If you can't detect the source of the leak and the smell continues, evacuate the building and keep all people at least two hundred yards from the cabin since there may be a leak in a propane line. Don't try to fix the problem yourself. Leave the area and contact the hut manager immediately.

NO SOLAR ELECTRICITY

The photovoltaic system is not foolproof. There may not be enough solar energy stored in the batteries to power the lights. In that event, use lanterns, headlamps or flashlights.

Lack of solar power can affect other systems in the hut, as well. Propane cooktops on timers won't work, and the vent fan for the composting toilet will stop venting. If the smell from the toilet becomes unpleasant, you might want to borrow an old trick from Victorian England when the aristocracy had to mingle with the unwashed masses. Soak a handkerchief or cloth in vinegar or another strong-smelling solution and hold it to your nose while using the restroom. Make sure to keep the toilet room door closed to prevent any disagreeable smell from wafting into the rest of the cabin.

OTHER BAD SMELLS

Other troubling smells may come from food which previous guests "forgot" to pack out. Once when we were trying to sniff out the source of a foul odor, we discovered a five-pound bag of rotting potatoes and a plate of mold-covered fettucine under the sink. Check around the hut to see if trash or food has been left somewhere. Also be sure sink drains are covered to prevent the release of septic gases.

Hut Crashers

Huts operate on the honor system. Unfortunately, some people take advantage of the system and crash the hut by using it without a reservation. If the hut isn't full, it may not be obvious that a group is poaching space. But when the hut is full, it's easy to determine who is supposed to be there by the confirmation letters posted on the bulletin board. Don't hesitate to ask for proof of reservation from each group. Peer pressure is the strongest deterrent against hut crashing.

Scott Messina of Aspen Alpine Guides, a long-time user of huts, says: "You have to be a diplomat because every situation is different. If there is enough daylight left, I ask them to head out. If they're prepared for winter camping, I remind them that they must be a quarter mile from the cabin. If weather or nightfall requires that they stay in the cabin, I tell them that the huts do not have an open-door policy, that everyone else made a reservation and paid to stay there, and it would be nice if they did the same thing. I'll ask them to contact 10th Mountain and pay up when they get out. If their reaction is belligerent, I threaten to call the sheriff. The way I figure it, there'll always be 'scammers', and their bad karma will catch up with them sometime."

David Schweppe, operations manager for 10th Mountain Division Hut Association says that he makes friends with the crashers. He finds a time to speak privately with them about the hut system, and to tell them that everyone else paid, and the system only works if everyone plays by the rules. "I make them feel guilty. They usually pay when they get out," he explains.

Hut poachers are stealing services from the hut system. Unless it's getting late or if the weather is bad, you're entirely within your rights to ask the poachers to leave or to at least sleep on the floor if there's a shortage of beds.

Break Ins and Vandalism

If the hut has obviously been damaged or tools are missing, report it immediately to the hut system manager. You may be able to temporarily fix some of the damage yourself; duct tape, newspaper, and foil can seal a broken window if it isn't too windy. Contact the hut system manager about problems or suspicious activities. The hut manager will ask for your name, address, and telephone number, especially if law enforcement officers will need to follow up on information regarding criminal activities.

ANIMALS

Those cute critters that take peanuts out of your hand may also carry rabies or other disease. Although you may imagine that they're hungry and cold, remember they're in their natural environment and can fend for themselves. Please don't feed the animals or birds at the huts.

A large part of the hut experience is to be self-sufficient and that also applies to dealing with problems at the huts. You may need to be ingenious and resourceful to have a successful hut experience.

IN THE KITCHEN

"Wilderness. . .is more than ever the last
refuge of the raw sensualist. . .the
place where we taste experience. . ."
—*Bob Shacochis,*
Outside Magazine,
July 1996

Much of the planning that goes into a hut trip revolves around food, and some of the fondest memories of a hut trip involve food and the companionship of sharing a table. All you need is basic sustenance and companionship, but most hut travelers make up for the weight they save by not needing to carry tents and cooking gear by bringing gourmet meals and bottles of wine.

Dinner with friends and hut hosts after successfully completing the 10th Mountain Interconnect, January 1996. Photo by Maryann Rowley

In this chapter, we discuss meal planning and preparation, food safety, trash management, dish-washing techniques, and how to get water. If you plan in advance to keep meals simple to use as few dishes as possible, and to minimize the trash you generate, you'll be happier trippers.

TYPICAL HUT KITCHENS

A typical hut kitchen is well supplied with pots and pans, cast-iron skillets, stockpots, dishes, mugs, glasses, utensils, cutlery, dish soap, and paper towels. You won't find a salmon poacher, asparagus steamer, or espresso maker. A few huts may have a wok, but most won't. If a birthday or special occasion requires a special meal, plan to bring the cookware you'll need with you.

KITCHEN KIT

It's a good idea to bring some of your own supplies to the hut. A list of items you might want to include in your kitchen kit are: salt and pepper, oil, matches, rubber gloves (to protect your hands from the necessarily hot dish-washing water), an apron (to protect your expensive fleece), bleach (to disinfect dishes), soap, a dish towel (you'll be lucky if the hut has a clean one), aluminum foil, and extra Ziploc bags (for trash, leftovers, wet clothes, etc.).

A moment alone and a cup of tea at Francie's Cabin, Colorado. Photo by Todd Powell

Food

Meal Planning

You'll be burning calories like a steam locomotive, so plan meals that are high in complex carbohydrates. Bring more food than you'd eat at home; you'll want larger servings for your heartier appetites. However, don't bring too much food; you don't want to have to carry it out since you can't leave it behind. Meal planning will be easier if everyone in the group brings their own lunches and snacks and you plan on group meals for dinner and breakfast.

One of the nice things about a winter hut trip is that it gives many more food options than summer, when you have to worry about spoilage. Warm spring days should be a concern, though; food can heat up fast in a dark-colored pack on a sunny trail. Some tips for food safety: avoid uncooked poultry and mayonnaise, use canned or dried meats for the second and third days unless you can count on the weather being cold, and don't expose your pack to direct sunlight.

Food Preparation Before Your Trip

Prepare as much as possible at home. Clean, trim, and slice vegetables, remove excess packaging, and re-package food in zip-lock bags. Grate cheese, slice and butter bread, bake potatoes, chop garlic and onions, and mix dry ingredients that you'll use for baking. If you're having spaghetti, chili, Stroganoff, stew, or other toppings for pasta or rice, make the sauce ahead of time, portion it out, package it in double Ziploc bags, and freeze it. It will travel well and you'll save time at the hut.

Food For The Trail

Complex carbohydrates that are easily digested provide a lot of energy, travel well, and are ideal for the trail. Energy bars, dried fruit, trail mix, bagels, granola bars, chocolate, crackers and cheese, in addition to hard meats such as salami, are good trail foods.

Meal Planning for a Multi-night Trip

You'll need more food for a longer trip, so bulk and weight are important considerations. Pack as much nutrition as you can into the least possible bulk and weight. Tortillas, grains, rice, couscous, pasta, and dried potatoes are all good backcountry foods. Freeze-dried meals are great if you'll be on the trail for a long time. Ramen noodles and seasonings are about as light as you can get. Plan to eat fresh foods and vegetables the first few nights, then move on to dried foods like rice and potatoes as your trip progresses.

Kitchen wizardry helps in the backcountry. Photo by Brian Litz

Some Favorite Menus

We like fast, easy breakfasts: instant oatmeal, hot cooked cereals, fruit, granola bars, bagels, and quick breads.

Snacks are an important part of an enjoyable hut experience. Cheese and crackers travel better than chips and salsa. Most supermarkets carry a wide variety of trail mixes. Smoked oysters on crackers make an elegant hors d'oeuvre. Jiffy Pop cooked over the woodfire or propane cooktop is as fun and satisfying as it is easy to carry.

Spaghetti is a hut dinner classic, but gets tiresome after too many trips. Stir-fried vegetables on quick rice, burritos made with dried bean mix, pizza (if there's an oven), and pre-made chili, stew, or Stroganoff are all good hut foods. Pre-washed and packaged lettuce is perfect for a hut trip, but carry it inside your parka in freezing weather or it may turn crisper than you would like. Dessert can be as simple as a chocolate bar, but in winter you can even enjoy ice cream or other frozen treats.

Avoid fruits that bruise easily and meats that require grilling, because grills at the huts are rare, especially in winter.

PLANNING FOR MINIMAL TRASH

Trimming your vegetables, re-packaging foods, and preparing sauces in advance cuts down on the trash you generate and have to pack out when you go. Re-package canned foods into Ziploc bags. Bring soda or beer in aluminum cans that can be crushed. The thin plastic water bottles used to package commercial spring-water are great for liquids such as wine or soy sauce; after they're empty, you can crush them flat. Some people prefer to bring wine that comes in a box. They leave the box at home, and bring only the inner wine bladder. It may not be the best wine you ever had, but sometimes you have to consider weight and waste over taste.

COOKING AT THE HUT

Cooking at the hut will be different than cooking at home, in part because of the difference in altitude. High altitude is considered to be any elevation over 4,500 feet. Water boils at a lower temperature and food takes longer to cook. At huts in the 11,000 foot range, water boils at 190° F (88° C) or less. Keep lids on pots, and water will boil faster. Pasta and rice can take two to three times longer to cook than they do at sea level.

Use couscous, instant brown rice, or Minute rice for speedier cooking. Capellini (angel hair) pasta cooks in a fraction of the time it takes to cook other pastas. Use lots of water when cooking pasta or it will turn into something resembling wallpaper paste.

Coffee is a morning necessity for many people. The huts may have old fashioned percolators or you can make cowboy coffee by boiling ground beans. Just don't expect espresso, unless you bring the maker yourself.

Pancakes are popular for breakfast, but they take a long time to make and generate a lot of messy dishes. Dry pancake mixes that require only water (such as Krusteaz or Hungry Jack) are easier to prepare because you don't have to bring eggs or oil. Cook all pancakes ahead of time—it's easier to transport cooked cakes than it is to carry raw batter. Never pour batter down the sink; it gums up the drain.

Eggs carried in a camper's plastic egg container won't break along the trail, but you'll have to deal with the bulky empty container, and carry home the egg shells. We recommend cracking the eggs into a crushable plastic container at home. That way you minimize bulk and trash at the same time.

Using a Wood-burning Stove

One of the more novel hut experiences is preparing meals on a wood-burning cookstove. There is an art to it. It takes time to learn how much wood the stove needs, where in the firebox to place the wood, where the stove's hot spots are on the cooking surface, and how to regulate oven temperatures.

Starting a fire in a woodstove and keeping it going can be difficult, and it is always time consuming. The key to cooking on a woodstove is to use small, even-size pieces of wood, and to tend the fire constantly.

The woodstove firebox is small and is built on top of an open grate that filters ashes. To start a fire in the firebox, use a lot of paper, small pieces of wood, and a lot of patience. Keep feeding the fire small pieces of wood until you have a good base of embers, then add larger pieces. Adjust the dampers to keep the air flowing and the fire burning. Avoid giving the fire too much air or it will burn too hot and burn itself out.

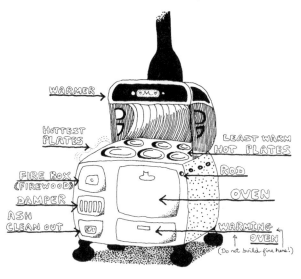

WOOD COOKSTOVE

A fire in a wood-burning stove burns down quickly, so you need to stay close to feed the flames. Unlike your oven at home, you can't put a lasagna in to bake and then head out to the garden for an hour.

Use the hottest plates nearest the firebox for boiling water and high-temperature cooking. The hot plates farthest from the firebox are best for simmering.

If you are having difficulty lighting a fire, line the bottom of the firebox with paper towels to keep the crumpled newspaper and small pieces of wood from falling through the grate until your fire gets going. Sometimes the grate or tumblers in the firebox will come out of their support bracket, making it impossible to light a fire. It takes a contortionist with long arms, reach up from the ash clean-out, to reposition the grates.

Baking

If you want to bake, you'll need to adjust the stove damper to draw heat to the oven. It takes about an hour to get the oven warm enough for baking, so plan ahead. It's wise to plan a meal that doesn't require baking on your first night at the hut. You may have problems on the trail and arrive late, and you'll be in no mood to wait an hour or more just to get your dinner in the oven.

The simple pleasure of baking a fresh batch of homemade cookies in a wood-burning stove is one of the joys of hut tripping. Because you're baking at high altitude, you'll need to adjust your recipe to lower air pressure and humidity. Use more flour and liquid, and less leavening in your mix— quantities depend on how high you are. If you're using a store-bought mix, consult the directions on the package for high-altitude adjustments.

If you plan to make cookies at the hut, consider preparing the dough at home. You can wrap the dough in waxed paper or foil and freeze it for the trip to the cabin. You'll save a lot of time and mess at the hut if you pack in the dough. If you want to mix the ingredients at the hut, measure the dry ingredients and package them beforehand in a Ziploc bag.

Watch cookies and other treats carefully while they bake. The oven thermometer may not operate correctly. To help with the uneven heat common in wood-burning stoves, gently cover your baked goods with aluminum foil. Remove the foil during the last five minutes for browning.

Using Propane Systems

Propane cooktops at huts give you more options than you'll have with a woodstove alone. It's easier to control cooking temperatures and to boil water with propane. Extra cooktop surfaces also ease the kitchen crunch when many groups are cooking at once.

Liquid propane is highly flammable and should be treated with caution. Children should never be allowed to operate propane cooktops. A quick and steady hand (or two) is required to hold the safety valve, turn

Dinner usually begins with boiling water. Photo by Leigh Girvin Yule

on the burner, and light the stove. Propane is difficult and expensive to bring into the huts, so use it sparingly. Avoid melting snow on the propane cooktops unless you are in need of water.

Each propane system is different, so you'll need to review the instructions posted near the cooktops. Have your headlamp handy for cooking in the evening so that you can read the stove instructions. There are two types of propane systems: those with a safety valve, timer, and/or thermocouple and those without. The more complicated systems that use safety valves and timer switches and a thermocouple are designed to shut off automatically to conserve propane. Whenever the thermocouple gets too hot from over use, the propane cooktop shuts off.

Some cabins have a timer switch linked to the photovoltaic system to limit the amount of propane that can be used. Be sure the photovoltaic system is turned on so that the timer can work.

Many propane stove knobs break because guests force them. Be sure to push knobs in, and turn them counterclockwise. We've visited huts where only one knob was left to operate all of the cooktops. You'll need pliers or strong fingers to turn the brass pin where a knob once was, or you can move the remaining knob around to the various burners.

If the thermocouple gets too hot it will shut off the system. A simple fix is to move the thermocouple away from the flame. Experiment with different positions and be sure to move the thermocouple gently because it's only attached by a thin, copper wire.

If the propane supply is depleted, which can happen late in the season or because the photovoltaic system has no energy to power the timer, cook on the woodstove. Otherwise, cook outside with the camp stove you brought with you for an emergency.

If there is a propane leak, you'll smell it. Propane is treated with the same nasty smelling additive as natural gas in order to alert you to a leak. Most likely, someone has left one of the burners on.

THE ART OF DISH-WASHING

The art of hand-washing dishes has nearly disappeared in this age of automated dish-washing machines. This can be a problem at the huts where you have no choice but to wash dishes by hand. And you must do a good job of it, too, to prevent diseases from spreading.

While you're finishing your meal preparations, put a large pot of water on the stove to heat for washing dishes. Scrape leftovers from dirty dishes into a trash bag. Set up two dish-pans: one dish-pan has hot, soapy wash water, the other has warm, clean rinse water and a splash of bleach (enough to give a distinct odor of chlorine). Set out a pitcher of clean water for a final rinse.

Wash and scrub dishes thoroughly in *hot,* soapy water. High heat is important to clean and sanitize dishes. Use your rubber gloves to protect your hands. Double rinse. You won't want your first sip of morning coffee or tea to taste like soap. The first rinse is in the dish-pan with clean water and bleach. As items are taken out of the rinse water, pour clean water over them as though you were rinsing them under a faucet with running water.

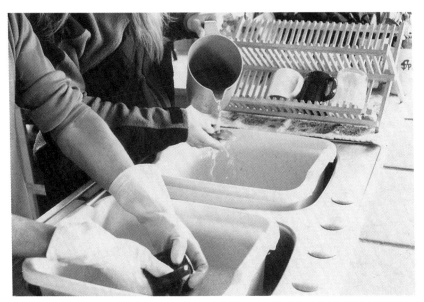

Washing dishes as a team. Photo by Scott Toepfer

Sink Etiquette

In many huts, the sinks are connected to a gray-water leach field that can handle biodegradable, liquid waste. It is alright to put dishwater, toothpaste, and clear liquids down the drains; but no grease, food particles, hair, or gloppy leftovers like stew, spaghetti sauce, or pancake batter should go down the drain. Pack those out with your other trash. In the more rustic hut systems, there is no sink drain. You strain out the food particles and toss the water outside the cabin, away from snow collection areas. Be sure to read any signs pertaining to use of sinks.

Since you can't wash food down the drain or throw it out on the snow—not only will it contaminate the snow, it also attracts animals—you'll need to strain your dishwater. Most hut sinks have a typical sink strainer that stays in the drain to collect food particles. If your hut doesn't have a strainer, fashion your own from metal mesh strainer or a dishcloth.

The Best Way To Deal With Grease

Make a cup out of aluminum foil. Pour your grease into the cup and put it outside until the grease hardens. In this way you can carry the solid grease out with your trash. In summer and fall it's not so easy. You can't put the grease outside the hut because it may attract bears or other unwanted furry guests. Put it in a container with a reliable lid that will keep it from spilling in your pack as you're heading out to the trailhead.

Packaging trash into small bundles. Photo by Todd Powell

TRASH MANAGEMENT

If you carefully plan meals to generate as little trash as possible, your food trash will be easy to manage. Never leave food, glass, wine bottles, or any trash at the huts.

- Burn what you can, but don't burn toxics such as plastic, cellophane, or aluminum foil. These products should go into your traveling trash-stash along with your food leftovers.
- For regular trash, double a Ziploc bag or other small trash bag. If you've done a good job planning, each person will only fill one quarter to one half of a large size Ziploc bag per day.
- For wet and messy trash, such as coffee grounds and leftover sauces, keep a separate Ziploc bag inside your regular trash bag.
- If your group is small, you can put aluminum cans, foil, and other recyclables in your doubled trash bag and sort it at home. For a larger group, a separate bag for the recyclables works better.
- Separate clean and reusable bags from dirty bags so you can use the clean ones for leftovers, lunches, or anything else you may want to put in a bag. Do not leave plastic bags behind; no one will want to use them because they won't know what they have been used for.
- Each person should have a personal trash bag (a small Ziploc bag is usually sufficient) in their toiletry kit. It can be used for dental floss, toilet paper, and loose hair from your hairbrush.
- Keep your trash bags small and manageable. It's easier to distribute eight small trash bags among the members of your group than it is to haul out one large, bulky one. Bundle up bags before they get too full, or they'll be too cumbersome to carry.

KITCHEN ETIQUETTE AND COURTESY

The kitchen can be the greatest source of aggravation among guests in different groups. Kitchen hogs who use every pot, pan, and cooktop in the hut, and don't wash their dishes promptly are the scourge of the hut experience.

For a positive kitchen experience, communicate your plans for mealtimes with other groups using the hut. Keep meal preparations simple and short, don't spread your stuff all over the counters, wash dishes as soon as you use them, and share your resources. Some Appalachian Mountain Club huts have kitchen sign-up times to manage the rush that inevitably occurs at mealtime. Treat the kitchen as you would a backcountry campsite, leave it cleaner than you found it.

FROM THE LOGBOOK

How nice it was to be greeted by a wonderful group of people who said, "If you like Indian food, don't even think of cooking dinner tonight!"

OF MICE AND MEN

If you don't want frequent encounters with mice, keep the kitchen clean, wash your dishes promptly, sweep up crumbs, and clean the kitchen surfaces after every meal. Always put your food away at night. Many huts provide plastic bins for temporary, mouse-proof food storage.

RHAPSODY IN FOOD

For someone who settles for Top Ramen and powdered Gatorade on any wilderness trek, I was astounded at the food cache we had divvied up to pack into the hut: frozen spaghetti sauce, pasta, salad fixings, loaves of sourdough bread, butter, fresh garlic, even a few bottles of red wine.

Once we reached the cabin, we greeted the two groups of strangers who were already there. We made our formal introductions and settled into our three "camps," separated by the immense expanse of the cabin's wooden floor.

When the last ray of light faded behind the mountains, the groups all migrated toward the kitchen. Some of our food had already been unpacked: spaghetti noodles, a tomato. Then someone asked, "You guys doing spaghetti?" "Yeah, you too?"

"Yeah. . .uh, if you want, we could all pool our food and make a really good dinner. . . ."

Everybody began pulling food from their backpacks, and all of us were probably thinking that the other group's food wouldn't be up to par. Then I saw the blue-cheese dressing. And croutons! "Why didn't we think of that? Mushrooms, great idea. Bell peppers!"

Soon the kitchen was abuzz with strangers working together, chopping, mincing, and all the while chatting like old friends.

That dinner was incredible, made more so by our pooling of talents. We not only had a great dinner, we made new friends. The wide expanse of the cabin floor was never again a void that weekend. We hunkered down together by the woodstove, shared stories, played a few games of cribbage—and even made a few turns on the hill with our new friends.

— Jane Stebbins, Breckenridge, Colorado

WATER

Snow is the source of all water at the huts, whether it's from snowmelt, groundwater, or creek run-off. That's why it's imperative to keep the snow around a cabin clean. One of the reasons dogs aren't allowed at the huts is the obvious problem of yellow snow. Just say no to yellow snow. Always use the outhouse. Never toss dishwater, ashes, floor sweepings, cigarette butts, or anything but snowballs onto the snow outside the cabin.

Collecting Snow

Collect snow in buckets or big, plastic trash cans identified by the hut manager for the purpose of storing snow. Most huts will not have a designated snow-collection area because there can be no guarantee that the snow in any given area will remain clean. When looking for a place to collect snow, go away from the cabin and away from signs of humans or animals. Drifts can be a good place to collect snow. Avoid gathering snow from the leeward side of the cabin where minute particles of ash from the woodstove settle. Snow can be heavy, so two people may be needed to carry the filled containers.

Making Water

It's not just God or Mother Nature who can make water. You can, too, by melting snow. Melting water from snow is time-consuming and labor intensive. You need large quantities of snow to make enough water for cooking, drinking, and washing. Dry powder snow melts into a whisper of water; the one time we bothered to measure, our twelve quarts of snow melted down to three and a half quarts of water—a ratio of about four to one. The process took more than an hour. Two thirsty trekkers can easily consume three and a half quarts (fourteen cups) of water in an afternoon. Melting water is a major hut activity if your group is to stay well hydrated.

To melt snow, place what you've gathered in a pot on the woodstove. Place a small amount of water in the bottom of the snowmelt pot to hasten melting. Without water in the bottom of the pot, the snow may burn off or evaporate before it melts. As the snow melts, add more to the pot. Keep collecting new snow. You'll need a lot more water than you think, and you'll need to leave some water for the next group.

If you need water fast, put smaller pots filled with snow on the woodstove. A smaller quantity of snow melts faster. Keep lids on the pots for faster melting.

To Treat or Not To Treat?

Many people go blithely through life drinking melted snow. To countless wilderness lovers, the backcountry would be a sad place if we couldn't drink melted snow from a fresh, mid-winter blizzard. But like creek water, snow can host an array of live organisms including algae, snow fleas, and *Giardia lamblia*, a parasitic organism that causes dysentery. These organisms are especially concentrated in the spring snowpack.

There are three easy ways to purify snow water—boil it, filter it, or treat it with iodine or chlorine. The long-held rule of thumb for purifying water was to bring melted snow to a hard boil and continue boiling it for two to three minutes at sea level, adding one additional minute for every 2,000 feet of elevation. That means you boil water for eight to nine minutes at 11,000 feet. Recent studies indicate that boiling water for so long may be unnecessary, however. *Giardia* cysts are shown to be inactivated immediately by boiling water. For a wide margin of safety, many experts suggest boiling water for three minutes at high altitudes. The drawback to boiling water is that it takes fuel and time. It can also make the water taste flat, and you're left with hot water to drink.

The water filter you bring along on your backpacking trips should work well for filtering snowmelt and creek water at the huts. You'll need a system that filters eight to twelve microns, the size of a *Giardia* cyst. No filters available in the United States claim complete virus removal. Only proper maintenance of filters will retain their effectiveness.

Treating water with iodine takes care of most parasites but makes the water taste terrible. Effective iodine treatment depends on the temperature of the water and duration of contact with iodine crystals. Follow all package directions carefully. Treating water with chlorine has proven to be less than 100 percent effective against *Giardia lamblia*.

What About Creek and Lake Water?

If creek or lake water isn't frozen you won't have to melt snow, but you may have to go a mile or more to fetch it. Water is heavy; it weighs about eight pounds per gallon. The best way to transport water is to carry it in a water backpack provided by the hut system manager or in two equal-size buckets so that you can distribute the weight evenly on both arms. Bring a scooper for dipping into the creek or lake and bring a friend to help you carry the load. Make sure that the buckets you use to transport water are clean.

Always treat creek and lake water. Protozoa such as *Giardia lamblia* and *Cryptosporidium,* bacteria like *Escherichia coli* and *Salmonella,* and viruses like Hepatitis A., can be found in most water systems in wilderness and recreational areas.

Hut Well Water

Some huts have hand-pumped wells like those you might find at a campground. Due to strict laws regarding communal water sources, many hut managers can't say that their well water is potable—even if it really is. Use well water only for washing dishes, cleaning, and bathing. See instructions near the pump for more information.

Cisterns

Snowmelt and rain collected from the roof may be stored in cisterns under a hut and brought up to the sink by use of a hand pump. This water is for washing only; it should not be used for cooking or drinking, even if it's treated.

TIPS FROM EXPERIENCED HUT-TRIPPERS

Save your pasta-cooking water for dish washing by straining your noodles over a dishpan.

FITTING IN

*Manners are the happy ways
of doing things.*
—*Ralph Waldo Emerson
(1803-1882)*

One of the greatest pleasures of staying at a hut can be meeting new people and making new friends. You'll probably share a meal, ski together, compare notes on other huts, divulge favorite ski runs, and discover that you have friends and interests in common. "Ah, what a small world," you'll say, and smile.

But sometimes other hut guests can be the source of your greatest frustrations and problems. Log books attest to drunken partiers; large, rowdy groups who dominate the cabin; rude and unsupervised children; and slobs who leave their food and trash behind. Some guests want to mix and mingle with their fellow hut inhabitants; others will keep to themselves. Cooperation, communication, and civility are keys to a successful hut trip when you share the cabin with others.

COMMUNAL LIVING

There is a certain etiquette to follow to live successfully with your fellow hut mates. It's part of the hut culture.
- Blend in.
- Practice the leave no trace ethic.
- Be as inconspicuous as possible.
- Be conscientious.
- Speak softly.

- Laugh gently.
- Don't draw attention to yourself except to set a good example by your actions.
- Occupy your space unobtrusively.
- Tread lightly.

Share the responsibility for collecting snow, melting water, tending the fire, chopping kindling, shoveling the decks, and all the other chores necessary for the hut to operate smoothly. Remember, you're all guests in an isolated cabin in the backcountry, and the cabin belongs to everyone.

When you arrive at the hut

- Brush snow and water off your clothing and boots before you enter the hut.
- Read and familiarize yourself with hut instructions posted at the check-in area.
- Post your confirmation letter promptly.
- Avoid wearing your boots inside the hut since they track in snow and mud. Boots are also noisy, especially on stairs.
- Don't spread your equipment and clothing all over hut.
- Don't monopolize the cabin and be especially sensitive to another person's space if your group is large.

At the trailhead. Photo by Leigh Girvin Yule

PARTIES AT THE HUT

Alcohol may be a social lubricant in some settings, but it can rub people the wrong way in others. Excessive drinking can be the greatest source of irritation among hut guests. Some people go to huts to let loose and blow off steam, but others go for peace and quiet. If you want to party, rent the entire hut; then you won't be imposing your party on others. Keep in mind that some huts have a separate hut-master's quarters, and partiers who rent the huts have no guarantee that they'll have the cabin to themselves.

For information about excessive drinking, hangovers, and safeguarding your health at huts, see Chapter 14, To Your Health.

Making music at the hut. Photo by Leigh Girvin Yule

MUSIC AT THE HUTS

Some people want complete quiet—to hear nothing but the crackle of the woodstove or the whisper of the wind outside. In our rapidly developing world, quiet places are disappearing. Amplified music, even if it's classical or recorded bird songs, is inappropriate in a hut unless your group has the hut to itself.

Acoustic music is less intrusive and more acceptable to most hut guests. We've enjoyed impromptu jam sessions courtesy of guests who brought up a cigar-box guitar, mandolin, and wooden spoons. Some huts have communal-use instruments. But the same rules apply to homemade music as to canned. Ask other hut guests if your music will bother them before you begin to play.

TEMPERATURE OF THE HUTS

People can get so worried about staying warm at night that they'll over-stoke the fire and make the cabin unbearably hot by bedtime. Not only does it waste firewood it also creates problems for people who don't wish to be so warm. Temperatures of 60 to 65° F (15° C to 18° C) are usually considered ideal for a hut, however you might want to keep the bedrooms cooler at around 50° F (10° C).

NO SMOKING PERMITTED

Smoking is not permitted in huts. If you smoke outside on the decks, be sure your smoke isn't bothering others. Cigarette smoke hangs in the air like diesel exhaust and pollutes the pristine environment. Never smoke around propane tanks or throw butts in the toilet. A lit cigarette can cause gases in the pit toilets to explode and can start a major fire in compost toilets because of the dry sawdust used in the toilets. Burn your cigarette butts in the woodstove or haul them out with your trash.

SLEEPING ARRANGEMENTS

Beds are taken on a first-come, first-serve basis; neither rooms nor beds are assigned. The most comfortable sleeping arrangements exist when each group takes a bedroom or a corner of the bunk room. Assume the cabin will be full and consolidate your group. Sleeping in the living area impedes the use of the room by other guests.

You'll often find a sheet already on a bed, but these sheets are placed there for comfort and aesthetics only. Linens are changed infrequently, sometimes only once a season. Think of your sleeping bag as your bed, but you may want to bring your own pillowcase.

Sleeping accommodations can be communal or relatively private. Photo by Pete Wingle

Snoring

One snorer can ruin a good night's sleep for everyone in the cabin and make enemies out of the best of friends. You can protect your sleep by using earplugs. If you're a person who snores, ask a friend to give you a quiet poke as soon as you start your nighttime serenade.

Quiet Time

Quiet time at the huts is generally from 10:00 P.M. to 7:00 A.M. so that everyone has a chance to get a good night's rest. If you're a night person, respect the quiet of others.

Romance

Dormitory-style lodging at most huts makes romantic interludes difficult at best. Even at huts with separate bedrooms, noise carries through walls, ventilation shafts, and windows. Few places are as romantic as the huts when you have one to yourselves, but it can be expensive to rent the whole cabin just to ensure your privacy. You may find that huts are usually the most quiet in December and April.

OWN YOUR OWN TRASH

Each group should keep their trash separate in order to avoid conflicts about who hauls what. No one wants to haul out another group's empty wine bottles or leftover dinner. Always pack out your glass and plastic containers.

CELLULAR PHONES

Your hut mates are probably in the backcountry to get a rest from phones, faxes, e-mail, and pagers. If you must bring and use your cellular phone, do so outside and away from other guests. Don't impose your technology on the simplicity of the huts.

SAUNA PROTOCOL

Some huts have saunas heated with woodburning stoves. Most saunas are small and can only accommodate a few people at a time. Sauna protocol dictates that the group who started the fire gets first dibs on the sauna. When the first group is all sauna-ed out, others get their turn. For more on using and enjoying a sauna, see Chapter 10, At the Hut and Chapter 14, To Your Health.

OUTHOUSE ETIQUETTE

At huts with just one outhouse, it's especially important to be aware of the amount of time you spend in the john, particularly during the morning rush. Two-hole outhouses and composting toilets are not separated into men-only or women-only rooms. Each bathroom is available to either sex. Be sure to leave the toilet clean for the next user—and don't forget to use the toilet flag.

"DON'T HARSH MY BLISS"

When your plans and expectations clash with those of other guests, try to talk about it with them. Seek out the other party's group leader and calmly convey your desires for the evening and ask if there's some compromise that can be reached to meet everyone's needs. Explain the expectations you had when you planned your trip. Try not to get angry or defensive as it may make the situation worse. If reason and goodwill don't work, take a deep breath, put in your earplugs, and try to make the best of it. Hope for better hut companions on your next trip or join the party!

LEAVE IT BETTER THAN YOU FOUND IT

Many guests want to help leave a hut in better condition than they found it. Hut managers are grateful for help shoveling the decks and stairs, splitting extra kindling, organizing kitchen pots and pans, tidying up the books and games, and any other type of general cleaning.

Should you leave water in the snowmelt pot when you leave? Some people say to pour out the leftover water so it won't freeze and crack its container. We believe you should leave snow and water in a metal pot on the woodstove so that the next group has water when they get there. They may be dehydrated and need water immediately. Check the hut instructions to see what the hut manager wants you to do.

TIPS FROM EXPERIENCED HUT-TRIPPERS

Bring something to share with other hut guests to help break the ice: homemade cookies, candy, an after-dinner liquor, a game, or your expertise in constellations, birds, animal tracks, photography, weather, avalanches, or other interesting subjects.

14

TO YOUR HEALTH

*Look to your health
...for health is a blessing
that money cannot buy.*
— *Izaak Walton (1593-1683)*

Nan and her friends arrived at their hut just after Christmas for a three-night stay. She started feeling poorly almost immediately, but brushed it off as the flu or a cold. By the second day she was bedridden, and by the third day she had a dry cough, was having difficulty breathing, and was lapsing in and out of consciousness.

Nan had lived at altitude and had even been a volunteer for a local search and rescue team, but neither she nor her friends, one of whom was a nurse, recognized the warning symptoms of Nan's deteriorating condition.

The third night Nan's friends finally decided to summon a search and rescue team. After midnight they dragged Nan on a sled through the cold, windy night to the top of a nearby pass where a helicopter was waiting to take her to a low-elevation hospital. It's lucky for Nan and her friends that they were able to get her out when they did, for Nan almost died of high altitude pulmonary edema (HAPE); her lungs had filled with fluid.

What might Nan and her friends have done differently? Had they been more aware of the many ways to protect themselves from altitude sickness, Nan might never have gotten as sick as she did. They might also have recognized the warning signs of Nan's condition earlier. Learning to take care of yourself and others in the backcountry by practicing prevention measures and becoming familiar with symptoms of serious illness will make you more confident, comfortable, and safe on a trip.

ALTITUDE

Western huts are located at elevations ranging from 8,500 to over 11,000 feet above sea level. Not only will you be exerting yourself physically just to get to the hut but you will be living and sleeping at elevations well above what you are accustomed to.

High altitude can cause a host of problems—headache, light headedness, dizziness, irregular breathing, fatigue, insomnia, loss of appetite, nausea, and swelling extremities. Often altitude sickness is mild, but as with Nan, it can also be life threatening.

Children and people who travel to the huts directly from lower altitudes are most prone to altitude sickness, and physical conditioning and living at higher elevations don't immunize a person from altitude sickness.

At over 11,620 feet, the Skinner Hut in Colorado's 10th Mountain Division hut system is one of the highest in North America. Photo by Brian Litz

Lower your chances of experiencing debilitating altitude sickness by following these preventive measures:

- Acclimate gradually by starting at a lower elevation and working your way to higher elevations over several days.
- Eat a high-carbohydrate diet and avoid salt prior to your trip.
- Hydrate! Drink lots of water before and during your trip.
- Avoid over-exertion. Pace yourself and rest frequently on the trail.
- When you arrive at the hut, eat small amounts of food at regular intervals instead of sitting down to one large meal.
- Take appropriate medications. See Chapter 15, First Aid and Rescue for more information on medications.

STAY HYDRATED

Drink lots of fluids before you leave for the trip, while on the trail, and at the hut. You should drink enough water to pass clear urine every one to two hours. If you feel thirsty, you're already dehydrated, since a person's sense of thirst lags behind their body's need for water. Water and sports drinks work the best to help you stay hydrated. Don't drink from streams unless you can properly treat the water. Avoid alcohol and caffeine. Alcohol is a diuretic, which makes you urinate more fluid than you take in and adds to your dehydration. Caffeine is a diuretic and a vasoconstrictor. Vasoconstriction is the body's defense against cold which, to ensure circulation of blood to the vital organs, restricts its flow to the extremities. Vasoconstriction is what makes our fingers and toes so prone to cold and frostbite.

TIPS FROM THE PROS

People lose a lot more fluid than they realize while exercising at altitude. Sweat evaporates more quickly in the dry air, and significant fluid loss occurs from more rapid and deeper breathing. Dehydration at altitude can be quite debilitating and compound the effects of Acute Mountain Sickness (AMS) and hypothermia.
—Christopher Pizzo, M.D.

It can be cold outside the hut. Here the windchill factor was near 30° F below zero. Photo by Scott Toepfer

COLD TEMPERATURES

A winter hut trip means that you have to deal with the cold. The heat you generate as you move along the trail keeps you warm and comfortable most of the time, but occasionally the weather will change or temperature drop so suddenly that you have to do more than just keep moving to stay warm. To help you stay warm in the high country when it's extremely cold, follow these tips:

- Stay hydrated to help the body fight cold and hypothermia.
- Wear a hat which helps keep your whole body warm since you lose most of your body heat through the top of your head, and cover exposed skin.
- Eat high-energy snacks such as chocolate or granola to create internal heat. Hot tea or soup from a thermos also helps to warm you up.
- Eat fatty foods the night before and the morning of a cold trip.
- Avoid alcohol, tobacco, and caffeine.
- Before you travel in the backcountry, educate yourself about hypothermia, frostbite, and altitude sickness. Know what to do if someone in your group shows signs of illness. See Chapter 15, First Aid and Rescue for more information.

PROTECT YOURSELF FROM THE SUN

Ultraviolet (UV) exposure from the sun is 40 percent higher at 10,000 feet than it is at sea level. When you combine the altitude with the reflective qualities of snow, the likelihood of severe sunburn increases. Use sunscreen with a sun protection factor (spf) of 15 or more. Sunscreen is absorbed best when applied to cool, dry skin at least thirty minutes before you go outdoors. Re-apply sunscreen every one to two hours, especially if you're sweating. UV rays reflect off the snow, so don't forget to put sunscreen on the underside of your nose, chin, neck, and ears. Choose a lip balm with sunblock in it. Zinc oxide, in traditional white or radical colors, is an effective total sunblock. Wear a hat with a wide brim.

TIPS FROM THE PROS

At higher altitudes, there is less atmosphere to filter out harmful ultraviolet radiation. No matter how tanned you are, or want to be, protect exposed skin with a sunscreen.

Cold sores are aggravated at altitude. If you're prone to cold sores, you may want to ask your physician to prescribe Acyclovir creme.

Snowblindness, sunburn of the eyes, is a risk even during overcast weather. Wear sunglasses or goggles with UV protection.

— Christopher Pizzo, M.D.

PREVENT BLISTERS

Blisters and hot spots are common on backcountry trips and may become debilitating. Take time to care for your feet. Tape or put moleskin on potential hot spots when you dress in the morning or before you head up the trail to keep blisters from forming. If you begin to develop a hot spot, stop immediately and tape it. An ounce of prevention is worth a pound of cure. If you have sweaty feet, tape and moleskin won't stick, so apply absorbent powder made especially for feet.

Most people use either a standard white athletic tape or moleskin for hot spots. Because of the coarseness of athletic tape, however, you may find that it rubs against your socks and contributes to blisters. Many people swear by duct tape. Its smooth surface precludes friction between socks and skin, and it sticks better than athletic tape or moleskin. Experiment with different tapes to find which one works best for you.

Carry products for blisters in your first aid kit, and be sure it's kept handy for easy access on the trail. A blister kit should contain: 1) athletic tape, duct tape, or moleskin, 2) callous "donuts" to protect blisters after they've formed, 3) Second Skin, Compeed, or a similar dressing, and 4) small scissors to cut tape, Second Skin, etc.

If you get blisters despite your best efforts to prevent them, protect them as you would a cut; guard against infection by applying an antibiotic ointment and cover them with a bandage. Allow the blister to dry if and when you're able. If it hurts to put on your boot, cushion the blister with a callous "donut," plenty of tape, and a dry pair of socks.

Protection from the sun can make for interesting headgear.
Photo by John Warner

Be careful not to overheat when skiing on a warm day. Photo by Scott Toepfer

WICK AWAY SWEAT

Physical exertion causes us to sweat even on the coldest winter days. Sweat can become icy cold as soon as we stop for lunch, to consult the map, or respond to a need for first aid. Chilled by our cold, sweaty clothes we may fall quickly into hypothermia.

Control your perspiration by managing your body temperature. Wear clothing made of wicking materials to draw perspiration out and away from your body. Start out on the trail cool; with exercise you'll soon warm up. Ventilate yourself by taking off a layer of clothes, hat, or gloves, and opening armpit zips and vent flaps before you get too hot and sweaty. Dress in light layers so you can remove them as necessary. Sometimes a polypropylene top is all you need under your jacket.

For sweaty feet use plenty of absorbent talcum powder made especially for use on feet. Baby powder has oil in the talc, which prevents tape and moleskin from sticking.

Your hands and head get sweaty and cold, too. Glove liners help wick moisture from your hands. Bring an extra pair of gloves and an extra hat or headband. Put wet gloves inside your jacket to help them dry while you're on the trail.

TIPS FROM THE PROS

Bring at least three pairs of socks—one for sweating up the trail, one for sweating while skiing and playing, and one dry pair for lounging around the cabin.
— *Mike Zobbe, Hut Master*

LOW HUMIDITY

The dry, high mountain climate can cause minor but uncomfortable health conditions. You can soothe dry eyes with eyedrops, and soothe a minor cough with teas or lozenges. A dab of oil or petroleum jelly in your nostrils will help keep mucous membranes from drying out and becoming irritated.

You may find that the dryness makes wearing contact lenses uncomfortable. Try removing and re-wetting them periodically and keep the lens case and eyeglasses handy should you decide to put your contacts away for the duration of the trip.

GASTRO-INTESTINAL DISTRESS

Travel to a hut and the change in diet can affect your digestive system. Gas also increases at higher altitudes. If you are someone with a delicate digestive system, remember to bring any personal remedies in your first aid kit.

Water from melted snow at the huts may also be a source of digestive disorders. Most of us drink chlorinated and purified bottled or city water in the course of our daily lives. Unlike that water, snowmelt water or hut well water contains a host of living organisms. Usually these organisms are harmless, but for the person whose body is unaccustomed to them the organisms can cause diarrhea, bloating, and gas.

PERSONAL CLEANLINESS

Dirty hands are one of the major ways that diseases are spread. Because there's no running water at the huts, wash your hands in a dishpan or sink basin with a small amount of water and a splash of bleach. Always dunk your hands in this solution before you prepare meals.

Bathing at the huts requires ingenuity. Photo by John Warner

For a good hand washing, you'll need a friend to act as the faucet. Fill a juice pitcher with warm water and have your friend pour it over your hands to rinse off the soap.

BRUSHING YOUR TEETH

Without a formal bathroom in the huts, you will be brushing your teeth in the kitchen with everyone else. If you are shy about it, go outside until you need to come in to spit and rinse in the sink. Just be sure some-one isn't cleaning vegetables!

MENSTRUATION

Women would be wise to learn from the Boy Scouts—be prepared. Travel can cause changes in your menstrual cycle, and it may come when you least expect it. (You won't find a Kotex dispenser in the outhouse!) Carry a toiletry kit with sanitary supplies, toilet paper, moistened tow-elettes, and a spare Ziploc bag for waste.

Never put tampons or pads in the toilet; pack them out with the rest of your trash. Put them in the same personal Ziploc bag where you put the toilet paper you've used on the trail.

GET YOUR SLEEP

Sleep is necessary in order to renew your energy for the next day, yet many people complain that they sleep poorly at the huts. They feel the altitude, are sensitive to noise, uncomfortable in unfamiliar surroundings, and worried about the blizzard raging outside. To protect your rest, avoid alcohol and caffeine, and drink warm milk, herbal tea or some other calming beverage before you go to sleep. Wear earplugs. We have a friend whose sure-fire method for sleeping at the huts includes a sleeping pill, earplugs, and a hat pulled down over his head to keep earplugs in and the light out.

ALCOHOL AND HANGOVERS

Drinking excessive alcohol at high altitude will give you one of the worst hangovers you've ever had. Even small amounts of alcohol have a greater effect at altitude—it takes less to get you drunk and less to make you feel bad the next day.

Alcohol consumption can make altitude sickness worse. It causes dehydration, and, in excess, may contribute to high altitude cerebral edema (HACE). See Chapter 15, First Aid and Rescue for more information.

Hangovers take time to cure, but a few things can help you feel better sooner: over-the-counter pain killers, such as aspirin, acetaminophen or ibuprofen; carbohydrates such as sugary and starchy foods; lots of water and/or sports drinks; and a long nap.

RODENTS AND HANTAVIRUS

It's virtually impossible to mouse-proof a backcountry cabin, but you can reduce problems associated with rodents by keeping the huts clean, by storing food in rodent-proof containers, and by remembering to take out all your food and trash when you leave.

Rodent droppings can carry disease. Hantavirus pulmonary syndrome is a disease that leads to rapid respiratory failure and possible death. Hantavirus has been detected at elevations as high as Craig, Colorado (6,186 feet). Symptoms include fever, headache, shortness of breath, severe muscle aches, coughing, vomiting, and abdominal pain. If you experience these symptoms within one to six weeks of exposure to rodents or rodent secretions, see your doctor immediately. The best treatment for hantavirus is early detection and hospital care.

Should you encounter rodents or their droppings in the huts, use special precautions. Wear rubber gloves, spray rodents and their droppings with a disinfectant or bleach solution, and dispose of cleaning rags, droppings, and rodents by double sealing them in a plastic bag. Wash rubber gloves before removing them and then wash your hands well. Do not sweep rodent droppings since the airborne dust can carry the hantavirus.

USING THE SAUNA

The sauna is a way of life in many cold countries and is rooted in ancient religious traditions hailing back to the human need for cleanliness. Many of the larger huts in Colorado have saunas, and they'll seem to travelers like a warm breath of life after their long, frigid trip to the cabin, or hard day of skiing in the cold. Remember that a sauna is no more private than is the hut. Use it, knowing that other people will be there, too. Because the use of clothing (even a swimsuit) is not usually expected in a sauna, be prepared to encounter naked strangers.

Guard your health carefully in the sauna. If you're feeling dizzy, light-headed, ill, nauseous, or if you find you are having difficulty breathing, get out of the sauna immediately. If you're on the verge of fainting, have someone help you out so that you're in no danger of collapsing into the fire or hitting your head. Be especially careful when moving about inside the sauna. You may feel fine sitting down but be overcome by light-headedness when you stand up.

Saunas should not be used by people with heart disease. People with any kind of health complication or concern (including pregnancy) should consult with their physician before using any sauna.

Sip water while in the sauna. Drinking beer or other alcoholic beverages will contribute to dehydration and dizziness. Using a sauna is serious business. Heat alone puts you off balance. Mix alcohol, a hot stove, and naked skin, and you could do serious damage to yourself.

Make sure you take a light source such as a headlamp or a lantern with you to the sauna (a candle will melt in the heat), and plenty of water to drink and splash on your sweating body. Leave anything made of metal, including jewelry and eyeglasses outside; they will burn your skin. Plastic eyeglass frames may melt, and contact lenses will be uncomfortable due to the sauna's dryness and heat.

One of our friends who read the first draft of *The Hut Handbook* said that he'd be afraid to go on a hut trip after realizing how many things could go wrong. We told him that to be forewarned is to be prepared for the worst and the best. Once you learn where danger lies, you're better able to avoid it. With attention to preventative care and precaution, you'll return to your home in better health and with a better appreciation of the simple life.

15

FIRST AID AND RESCUE

What we anticipate seldom occurs;
what we least expect generally happens.
—Benjamin Disraeli (1804-1881)

On a Super Bowl Sunday, Reece and his friends decided to go back-country skiing before heading to a local pub for a beer and the game. They skied past a hut still under construction on their way up to the powder bowls. After several turns, Reece hit a rock and fractured his leg. His friends skied down to the cabin and kicked in the door which was not yet fully framed. They found a piece of plywood that they could use to drag Reece from the slope to the cabin. A construction heater kept Reece warm while they waited more than three hours for the rescue team to arrive. "That cabin saved Reece's life," said the rescue-mission coordinator after they'd gotten Reece safely to a hospital. "His femur was broken in seven places!"

In this chapter we don't presume to make backcountry doctors out of you, or teach Red Cross Advanced First Aid, or emergency medical training. We aren't certified instructors, and we don't pretend to be so. We mention here only the basics: what you need in your first aid kit, symptoms and illness common to high altitudes, and a few of the various kinds of injuries common to outdoor recreation.

A few first aid emergencies—bone and joint injuries, hypothermia (dangerously low body-core temperature), Acute Mountain Sickness (AMS), or just plain altitude sickness, along with blisters, cuts and burns—are all more common in mountain environments. AMS, hypothermia, and trauma injuries are potentially life-threatening and must be dealt with rapidly.

Dr. Chris Pizzo, a respected climber and expert in altitude sickness, and Dale Atkins, U.S. representative to the International Alpine Rescue Commission contributed their experience and knowledge of backcountry first aid and rescue to this chapter.

HEALTH AND SAFETY TIPS FOR COLORADO HUT SKIERS

By **Christopher Pizzo, M.D.**

Many of the same features that attract people to the Colorado high country can cause problems for the ill-prepared. As you go higher, the barometric pressure decreases and less oxygen is available. It is colder, drier, and ultraviolet rays from the sun are stronger. Each of these changes can have unpleasant effects on your body and detract from the quality of your backcountry experience.

Most Colorado hut skiing occurs between 8,000 and 12,000 feet above sea level with access to altitudes even higher. More-rapid breathing, especially during exercise, is one of the first things people notice upon arrival at altitude and is one of the body's ways of adapting to a low-oxygen environment. If there's less oxygen in the air, you have to breathe harder to get your blood oxygenated in your lungs. If there is less oxygen in your blood, your heart will beat faster to deliver oxygen to your muscles and other metabolically active tissues. Normally, these are beneficial adaptive changes, but when the heart pumps too much blood to your brain, which lies inside an enclosed structure—the skull or cranium—it can result in increased intracranial pressure. It is this increased intracranial pressure which causes the symptom complex we refer to as acute mountain sickness (AMS). The most common and prominent symptom is headache. Typically, headache occurs within a few hours after ascent to a high altitude or upon awakening the next morning, because of a person's tendency to under-breathe during sleep. Other symptoms of AMS include nausea, insomnia, dizziness, and loss of appetite.

Reduced urination and other signs of fluid retention may also signal poor acclimitization. Studies have shown that as many as 30 percent of the visitors to Colorado ski areas, even at altitudes lower than our ski huts, show some of the signs and symptoms of AMS.

These symptoms usually go away in a day or two after acclimatization. Ascending to higher elevations while ill with AMS may be courting disaster; indeed, if symptoms persist or worsen, it's crucial to get down to a lower elevation. The development of a cough or more severe shortness of breath may signal onset of high altitude pulmonary edema (HAPE), which occurs when increased blood flow to the lungs results in a leak of fluid into the air spaces of the lungs, the alveoli. This condition is potentially fatal if oxygen and professional medical care aren't available. Moving to lower altitude may be life-saving. The same is true with high altitude cerebral edema (HACE) where there is a fluid leak into the brain. In addition to headache, people suffering from HACE lose coordination and fall in and out of consciousness.

You can do a few things to prevent AMS. If you live at sea level, spending a night or two at a modest altitude like Denver's 5,280 feet can help you with acclimatization. Eat foods high in carbohydrates. Drink lots of water. Avoid salty foods, caffeine, and alcohol. Diamox (acetazolamide) is a prescription drug which can prevent or treat AMS. It speeds the acclimatization process and stimulates breathing during sleep. Taking 125 mg twice a day starting a day before arrival at altitude will prevent AMS in most people. It cannot be taken during pregnancy or by people allergic to sulfa drugs. Since it is a prescription medication, you will need to discuss its use with your physician.

Another consequence of higher altitude is colder temperatures. Even with adequate clothing, including good hats, gloves, and boots, hypothermia can occur if you are wet, exposed to wind, tired, under-hydrated, or underfed. Warning signs of hypothermia include clumsiness, confusion, irritability, and cessation of shivering. If you suspect that you or someone else is hypothermic, stop in an area protected from wind, warm up, change out of wet clothing, eat carbohydrates, and drink. Tight-fitting and/or wet boots or gloves can cause frostbite. If there's a loss of sensation in fingers or toes, stop and look for numb, cold, white areas, and take time to warm them up.

Enjoying a Colorado hut experience requires avoidance of illness and injury. Remember that lack of oxygen can cloud judgment. Be conservative. Listen to your body and observe others.

Don't push yourself or others in the face of possible AMS, hypothermia, dehydration, hunger, or injury unless it is toward a reasonably accessible safe harbor. Stay safe, stay healthy, and have a great time.

COMMON HUT EMERGENCIES

Your injured friend's best chance of survival is you. Because outside help will take a long time to arrive, you'll need to stabilize the injured person. You may need to improvise splints, stop bleeding, or manage an airway to keep the person breathing. The first aid ABC's are Airway, Breathing, and Circulation, and you'll need to learn what to know about them by attending a first aid or mountain rescue course. Serious bleeding and the cessation of breathing are rare but can occur in the backcountry, so make sure you know how to respond to these emergencies before heading out.

In addition to broken bones, altitude sickness, and hypothermia, burns and cuts are accidents common to the hut experience. Burns are common because of the woodstoves and propane cooktops. A burn should be irrigated with cold water or covered with an ice or snow compress. Don't place snow or ice directly on the skin for prolonged periods of time; instead, place a towel or cloth against the skin before applying the compress. Keep the burn area clean to prevent infection. For more burn care information, refer to one of the wilderness first aid books listed in the bibliography.

Cuts are common hut accidents because people are using axes for kindling along with an assortment of sharp knives for everything from meal preparations to cutting duct tape. Elevate the wound and use compression to stop bleeding.

FIRST AID KITS

All huts have first aid kits, but some kits may contain only band aids; the group that was there before you may have needed to use everything in the first aid kit. For that reason, every member of a hut party needs his or her own first aid kit. The items listed below are first aid kit basics.

1. Pocket mask
2. Latex gloves
3. Sterile compresses
4. Wire splints for broken arms
5. Cravats for shoulder and arm injuries

A well-equipped first aid kit. Photo by Leigh Girvin Yule

6. Burn compresses for the more serious burns
7. Aspirin or ibuprofen for pain
8. Safety pins
9. Traction device for broken femurs
10. Small scissors
11. Roll of gauze for wrapping injuries
12. Moleskin for blisters
13. White first aid tape
14. Band aids
15. Ace bandage
16. A length of rope
17. Antibiotic ointment

Many mountaineering stores and catalogs carry basic first aid kits. Backcountry enthusiasts should give as much attention to their first aid kit as they do to their pack, boots, or skis.

EMERGENCY SLEDS

If someone in your group is injured and you believe you may be able to get him or her out of the backcountry without calling a rescue team, you'll need to devise a means of transportation. Use the person's skis to build a sled to get him or her to the trailhead. With a little ingenuity and a

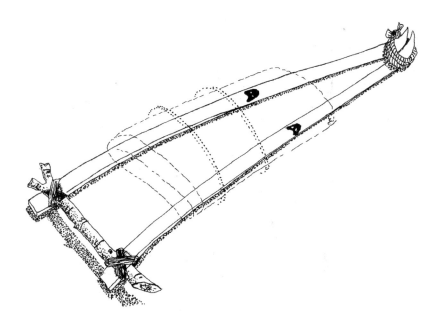

roll of duct tape, you can build an adequate sled to haul anyone out of the mountains.

If the skis have holes in their tips, hook them together with a carabiner or tie them together with a length of rope. Use duct tape to lash a ski pole or wooden stick across the ski tails in order to keep them about two feet apart. This becomes the main body of your sled. Then place a sleeping bag or blanket on top of the skis so that the injured person can sit or lie there. Secure the person to the sled with a length of rope so that he or she won't fall off. You'll also need to devise a handle for the front of the sled—maybe a pair of ski poles attached to the skis with a carabiner or rope loop at the front of the skis. Also attach a rope through holes at the back of the skis to provide additional handles to help control and pull the sled. Make sure your handles are secure so that the sled can't slide away from you. If your skis don't have holes at the tips and tails, use extra duct tape.

SEARCH AND RESCUE TEAMS

Sometimes calling a search and rescue team is your only option. If you're carrying a cell phone try 911, but you may not get a connection because cell phone service is extremely limited in remote areas. Usually someone, preferably two people will have to ski out to make the 911 call.

When Things Go Wrong and Outside Help is Needed

by Dale Atkins; U.S. Representative to the International Alpine Rescue Commission

Accidents happen to even the most experienced back-country travelers. Adverse weather (in summer or winter) or snow conditions can stop the strongest groups. What's worse is when sickness or injuries result in medical emergencies. In these cases prompt recognition of the problem and evacuation from the backcountry can mean the difference between life and death.

While the rescue dictum of all who venture into the backcountry is "self-rescue is the most reliable and quickest form of rescue," sometimes a party may not possess the equipment, strength, or skills to effect self-rescue, and an outside rescue team must be called.

In Colorado, as in most of North America, mountain rescue is usually performed by para-professional (highly-trained, volunteer) rescue teams. The members of a team train hundreds of hours each year, taking time away from their families and work, and finance their own equipment. They are ready to respond at any time. To ease the financial burden on rescue teams the State of Colorado may pay the cost of rescuing anyone in possession of a valid Colorado backcountry hiking certificate, or a hunting or fishing license.

The responsibility for search and rescue in Colorado rests with the county sheriff, who will usually turn the operation over to the local rescue team. Within minutes of a telephone call to 911 the leaders of the local team are notified and the team mobilized.

When to Get Help

Wise backcountry travelers know the importance of possessing a working knowledge of wilderness first aid, so they can distinguish between minor problems and those that may become serious ones. When in doubt, it is probably best to seek help from a trained rescue team. As Tim Setnicka writes in Wilderness Search and Rescue, *"Overreaction always seems justifiable; under-reaction always appears inexcusable."*

While the warmth and comfort of a hut is generally the best place to be with someone sick or injured, some conditions do require immediate evacuation. Pulmonary edema, unconsciousness, appendicitis, and a few other afflictions require that you begin an evacuation while rescuers travel to your aid. Evacuations of almost all other conditions such as head and neck injuries, heart attacks, stroke, and broken bones can usually wait until trained rescuers arrive.

Getting Help

Communications from the huts is not always possible. Even if you pack a cellular telephone you cannot expect it to work, so all parties should be prepared for the possibility of having to get messages out on foot. When cellular phones or small radios do work, you still should obtain all the information listed below before contacting the authorities. It is best to send two people out for help, but they should not leave the group or the injured person until it's certain their help won't be needed—until the situation is under control and adequate information about the victim and the group's plans are known.

The more information that reaches the rescue leader the more effective the rescue effort will be. To ensure that adequate information reaches the rescue leader, a written accident report must be completed. Sample forms can be found in books like Mountaineering: Freedom of the Hills, Mountaineering First Aid, and NOLS Wilderness First Aid. If the victim is not at a hut, a map with the victim's exact location pinpointed on it should accompany the report. If you don't have a form, here's the information you need to record (modified from Mountaineering First Aid):

- Name, age, address, phone number of victim, and who should be notified.
- When, where, and how the accident occurred.
- Number of persons, injured or ill, and the nature and seriousness of injuries.
- Condition of the victim and first aid administered. Include vital signs such as pulse and respirations from the initial exam and at the time the messengers left.
- Number of people, their equipment, and their general level of skill with the victim.

- *The party's exact location, and whether the members will wait or move to a more-readily accessible location.*
- *Weather conditions at the victim's location.*
- *Trail conditions (e.g., deep powder snow, packed trail, muddy trail, steep rocky area, etc).*
- *Names, addresses, and phone numbers of everyone in the party and whom to notify.*

One last thing: Be certain messengers have car keys. When the messengers reach a phone, contact the local sheriff's department by dialing 911. The person you talk to may not be rescue savvy, so be persistent and patient in communicating the information they'll need. Stay available; it's likely the rescue leader or a sheriff's officer will call you back for more information and to arrange a place to meet with you.

The rescue effort may appear slow to the victim and those waiting, but upon notification the first rescuers can generally be expected within a few hours to half a day. Remember that under some weather conditions it may take rescuers much longer or even prevent them from starting until conditions improve.

Helicopters

When available, the use of helicopters can save hours (or even days) of exhausting work by whisking the victim directly to the hospital. "When available" is an important phrase to remember. Never assume a helicopter will come to your rescue. Even if a helicopter is available, some weather conditions can and do prevent its use. If you are fortunate enough to have a helicopter come to your aid, here are some key things to remember:

- Let the pilot pick the landing site.
- Prepare possible landing sites. Remove or secure loose materials that might be blown into the rotor blades. Soft snow should be packed down.

- *Stay at least seventy-five feet away while the helicopter is landing. Almost always when helicopters land near a hut the pilot will shut down the aircraft, and a crew member will come to you. Only approach the helicopter after being signaled to do so by the pilot or crew chief.*
- *Always approach or leave the helicopter from the front so the pilot can see you at all times.*
- *Always approach or leave the helicopter from the downhill side.*
- *Never carry anything above your shoulders.*
- *Always follow the directions of the pilot or crew.*

Always go into the backcountry prepared for an emergency. Preparedness is the cheapest and best insurance there is. Have the knowledge, the ability to use it, and the proper equipment for first aid and backcountry evacuations. With proper caution, attentiveness, a little help from your friends, and luck with the elements, you'll probably never need to use them.

16

LEAVING THE HUT

...love that well which thou must leave ere long.

—*William Shakespeare (1564-1616)*

Imagine arriving at the hut. It's tidy and clean, and everything is well organized and stocked. The only traces of the previous guests are the glowing embers in the woodstove and their entry in the log book describing the wonderful time they had.

Wait a minute...this chapter is about leaving the hut, not arriving. We think that the way you leave a hut has something to do with the way you'll arrive at another. This chapter is about good hut karma. If you leave the hut in as good or better condition as you found it, your good karma will be returned to you with a beautiful, clean, well-stocked hut on your next trip.

How you leave the hut is one of the most important responsibilities you have as a hut user, and will affect the future success and viability of hut systems. If every guest takes good care of the cabins, cleans up, and hauls out their trash, the hut systems will continue to thrive for generations to come.

LEAVING THE HUT

Each hut system is different, and guest responsibilities may differ from system to system. Your check-out responsibilities will be posted along with the other hut instructions. Be sure to check them, so you'll know if there's anything special you need to do. A departure list will generally include the following tasks:

1. Clean up: Clean kitchen, wash and put away dishes, sweep floors upstairs and down, wipe surfaces, tidy cabin.
2. Haul out your trash.
3. Refill snowmelt pot with fresh snow.
4. Be sure all stove burners are off.
5. Let fire(s) burn down. Close woodstove doors and dampers.
6. Turn off circuit breakers at the loader center for photovoltaic system.
7. Lock all windows and doors and double-check to be sure. Spin the tumblers on the combination lock before locking it and tug on the lock to see if it holds.

Consider the needs of the group that arrives after you leave. They may be in trouble, they may have had problems along the trail, a member of the group may be injured or ill, or they may be arriving after dark. Hut etiquette calls for leaving the cabin stocked with water, kindling, and firewood. And the Golden Rule restated for huts is: "Leave the hut as clean for others as you would have them leave it for you."

If another group will be leaving the hut after yours, decide with them who will do what. Your group may chop the kindling and stock the firewood. The other group may sweep the floors and fill the snowmelt pot. Of course, each group is responsible for washing its own dishes, cleaning the kitchen, and hauling out its own trash.

If You Must Leave in a Hurry

If the weather is socked in, if you have to break through two feet of fresh snow, or if someone in your group is injured or sick, you may have to leave the cabin in a hurry. Usually, you'll know the night before that you must get an early start, and you'll be able to do your chores early. If an emergency requires you to leave so quickly that it's impossible to clean up as well as you should, leave a note for the in-coming guests to explain what happened. They'll be less upset when they find the cabin in disarray if they know it is the consequence of an unfortunate emergency.

If You Can't Leave

If foul weather prevents your group from leaving the hut, hunker down and wait out the storm. Chances are the group expected in that night will be hunkering down wherever they are, too, and won't make it to the cabin. But as soon as the storm is over, move on so that others with reservations can occupy the hut.

LOST AND FOUND

Valuables left at the huts rarely stay lost for long because most other hut-trippers will take them. There is always a chance that someone took what you've lost to hold for safekeeping until the rightful owner can be found.

If you've lost or found something at the hut, contact the hut manager and the reservations department (they may not be the same). If you've lost or found something along the trail, notify the hut manager, reservation department, the U.S. Forest Service, or the local sheriff's department.

CHECK-OUT TIME

In keeping with the casual nature of the hut experience, most hut systems don't have official check-out or check-in times. People usually arrive at the huts in the middle of the day because it takes most of the morning to get there. Hut etiquette calls for timing your departure and arrival for around 12:00 P.M. to 1:00 P.M. Some hut systems, such as the Summit Huts in Colorado, have an official check-out or check-in time of 1:00 P.M. With check-out and check-in time established, guests know when to expect the next group and what the deadline is for cleaning the cabins. Also, guests know they'll have privacy until 1:00 P.M. and won't have to feel rushed to leave first thing in the morning.

TIPS FROM EXPERIENCED HUT-TRIPPERS

If the hut is occupied when you leave, make sure the other group knows where the padlock or combination lock is so they can lock up on departure. (Francie's Cabin went unlocked for four days, one busy March because the padlock was lost.)

HEAVENLY EXERIENCE

Jennie wore her brand-new diamond earrings to Janet's Cabin, in Colorado, despite objections from her husband who gave them to her for Christmas. Before going to sleep, she took them off and put them on the shelf next to her bed. Of course, she forgot them the next morning when she left the cabin. She called Summit Huts Association in a panic, desperate for someone to go to the cabin to retrieve her valuable jewelry. SHA had no maintenance personnel scheduled for a week, so she offered to pay for a special trip. Needless to say, the diamonds weren't there when the hut master made it to Janet's Cabin the next day. But the story has a happy ending. The guest who stayed in the same bed the night after Jennie, found the earrings and took them with him on his travels to Fowler/Hilliard Hut for the next two nights. When he returned to civilization, he contacted the 10th Mountain Division Hut Association and turned in the earrings.

17

CHILDREN AT THE HUT

A happy childhood can't be cured.
—*Hortense Calisher (1911-   )*

Children can have a wonderful time at the huts, and it's a great way to introduce them to the backcountry, but bringing them requires careful planning and special sensitivity to other guests who may not be used to the din most children generate. Special planning includes deciding how to transport the children and the additional gear you'll need, ensuring your children's warmth, and taking into account their safety. Regarding sensitivity to other guests, families who rent the entire hut for themselves avoid potential conflicts with other hut users who may not understand your children's needs or appreciate their delightful and rambunctious energy.

GETTING CHILDREN INTO THE BACKCOUNTRY

There are two options for transporting children who can't hike or ski to the cabin on their own power. If a child is small enough to travel in a Snugli or backpack, you can carry the child. The drawback is that another adult often has to carry all the gear—including the extra sleeping bags, food, and clothing. Carrying a child in a backpack requires good balance because the adult will have a higher center of gravity. Furthermore, the risk of serious injury is also greater if the adult falls while carrying a child. The other option is to pull smaller children on a sled. Using a sled also gives you a way to transport the extra gear you need for children.

Regardless of how you transport children, you'll need to be attentive to hypothermia and other problems associated with cold temperatures. A child in a sled is essentially sliding in the snow and not generating any warmth through exercise. Similarly the child in a backpack, even though warmed by your body, is not generating the level of warmth that you are. You may be sweating and warm, while your child is becoming increasingly cold. Therefore, special precautions should be taken to be sure that the child is warmly dressed. In addition to warm clothes, chemical heat packs which warm up when exposed to oxygen are a good idea for children's sensitive hands and feet. Be sure to protect their skin by putting the heat pack between a glove liner and mitten, or between their socks and boots.

Small children who can ski or snowshoe to the cabin on their own will need a short, easy trail. Always have a plan of action, such as bringing a sled, in case the child needs a lift. Plan to travel slowly, and to stop frequently for snacks, sightseeing, and taking photographs. Pace yourself slowly enough for the children to keep up. Remember, when traveling in the backcountry with children, safety is paramount. Choose absolutely safe trails free from avalanche hazards, and always send an adult first to lead the group.

Family groups or single parent/single child pairs need an emergency plan in the event that the parent or responsible adult is hurt. Would the child be able to survive alone or effect a rescue? Parents who want to bring their children to the huts should consider going with other families in order to share responsibilities and avoid dangers too risky for one adult alone. Excessive cold, first aid, avalanches, and other backcountry hazards can be dealt with more easily with more than one adult. It's a good idea to have two adults per child.

One more point to consider—children are more susceptible to altitude sickness than adults. Be familiar with the symptoms of altitude sickness. For more information, see Chapter 14, To Your Health, and Chapter 15, First Aid and Rescue.

EDUCATIONAL PROGRAMS

More and more hut systems are offering educational programs for children. Mountain-area schools, recreational districts, and day camps make occasional forays to the huts. Taking part in these programs will give your children good backcountry experience. Ask the reservations department of a hut system about information on children's programs.

There aren't many leftovers after a long day in the backcountry. Photo by John Warner

FROM THE LOGBOOK

Thank you so much for the use of this cabin. I loved climbing Mt. Helen and seeing the white-tailed ptarmigan and sliding down the snow.
—C. G., age 12, California participant in Keystone Science School's On the Wing program at Francie's Cabin, Colorado.

HUT HAZARDS

The huts are full of potential hazards for children. We couldn't begin to imagine all the trouble that kids could get themselves into at the cabins, but here are a few obvious pitfalls to keep in mind:

- Huge stacks of firewood in the wood room may seem inviting to climb and play on, but the stack could easily topple and crush a child. Also, sharp axes, splitting mauls, and hatchets are easily accessible in the wood room.
- Stairs are potential hazards to small children because very few huts have doors or safety gates at the tops or bottom of the stairs.
- Children love to sleep on the top bunk bed, but they also have an uncanny ability to fall out of it.

- Hot stoves can be dangerous when children are rough-housing.
- Kitchens are never child-proofed. Cleaning fluids, bleach, sharp knives, and propane cooktops are easily within a child's reach.

WILDLIFE

Children are likely to be curious about the many different wild animals that live around the hut. Wild animals, however, are best left wild. Any animal that doesn't run away from even a small child is to be avoided. Rabies, bubonic plague, the hantavirus, and numerous other transmittable diseases are present in the backcountry. Never let children run off or wander around alone. They may be seen as prey to large predators, such as mountain lions, whose food source, along with their territory, is ever diminishing because of human encroachment.

ETIQUETTE

Children naturally get excited, rambunctious, and can make a lot of noise. Parents can help to keep their children reasonably quiet by bringing children's books and games (few huts supply them), going outside with them to play as much as possible, and keeping an eye on the children at all times. Remember that not all hut guests will have as much tolerance for children as you do. At night, a crying baby can be worse than a snorer for everyone but the child's parents.

In addition to helping children keep quiet, books, games, and other play items will enhance the good time they have at the hut. Don't forget about your children's comfort. If they need a high-chair or baby seat, you need to bring your own because huts don't supply them.

FROM THE LOGBOOK

We hiked a very long way to here from our car. But let me tell you it was worth it. My friend Marta and I are having a great time. We each got our own top bunk on the bunk bed.
    —C. M. T., age 10

This is my first time ever snowshoeing to a hut. I got to see the comet. It was the best time of my life.
    —A. G., age 9

18

SUMMER AT THE HUTS

*Summer afternoon—summer afternoon;
to me those have always been the
two most beautiful words in
the English Language.*
—Henry James (1843-1916)

The mountains in the summer reveal a different landscape than they do in the harsh winter months. Trails are easier to find, huts are easier to reach, and wildflowers, and wildlife abound in the high country.

Many people who would never consider a hut trip in winter will enjoy it in summer. Grandparents, small children, people with disabilities, and even couch potatoes will find the huts more attractive when they can drive a little closer once the snow is gone.

Seasoned winter hut users enjoy summer at the huts for the different options the warmer season offers them in hiking, fishing, climbing nearby peaks, sunbathing—or just hanging out in clothing other than fleece, wool socks, and ski hats.

People who don't like summer camping are often enamored with the hut experience; they get a bed, roof over their head, floor, toilet, and refuge from rain, lightning, large hailstones, and mosquitos. But despite the relative luxury of a hut, summer guests still have a backcountry experience packing in all their food and gear and enjoying their days on the trail.

Summer use calls for strong backcountry ethics to help counter the concerns of hut detractors discussed in Chapter 1. In this chapter, we'll cover those ethics, as well as discuss some of the important differences between summer and winter hut trips.

Summer is a great time to bring children to the huts. Photo by Scott Toepfer

SUMMER ACCESS

In Colorado, some huts and yurts are open during a few months of the high mountain summer, while elsewhere, huts are open year round. Because cold and snowy weather can last from October to June, the months for summer hut trips are usually July, August, and September. Inquire with your reservationist for hut schedules.

Even in summer when roads requiring high-clearance, four-wheel-drive vehicles are thawed and open, the huts still offer a non-motorized experience. The preferred access is to hike or mountain bike to the huts. You may not be able to get anywhere near the hut with a vehicle, and you'll have to schlepe your gear for a quarter mile or more. At other huts, motorized vehicles are not allowed at all. Don't count on help from horses or mules as they are rarely permitted at the huts.

REFRIGERATION AND FOOD SAFETY

In winter anything that needs refrigeration gets put into a snowbank, but summer snowbanks are difficult to find south of Canada and below 13,000 feet. Meal planning for a summer hut trip requires that you adjust for the lack of refrigeration. Groups able to drive near the cabin have the luxury of bringing in a cooler full of ice, but others will have to plan as though on a backpacking trip.

For the first night, you can eat meals you have frozen at home, such as meats and sauces. Insulate them well with crushed egg cartons and newspaper, keep them on ice until you get to the trailhead, and then store them deep in your pack. Or, you can freeze water in plastic bottles, place perishables between the bottles, and wrap them well with newspaper. When the ice melts, the cold water is a refreshing bonus.

WATER

In winter, water is easy to come by since you're surrounded by snow—you just shovel it into a pot and melt it. In summer you may have to carry water from a nearby spring or stream for drinking, washing, and cleaning. At some cabins you may have to hike nearly two miles to the nearest source of water. Another option is to pack in water from home. Remember, if you do use spring or stream water for drinking, you should filter or boil the water. See Chapter 12, In the Kitchen, for purifying tips.

Hut users pack their trash out with them when they go. Photo by Leigh Girvin Yule

OUTDOOR FIRES

Some huts have outdoor fire pits that can be used for cooking or simply enjoying a summer night accompanied by the flames of a campfire. Many huts don't have fire pits, however, because of concerns for wildlife and wildfire.

INSECT PESTS

Whoever said there are no mosquitos in the high country never spent a summer in the Rocky Mountains. Mosquitos can be so thick they'll drive you inside on the most beautiful of evenings. Protect yourself from insect pests by bringing an effective bug repellent. Ticks carrying Lyme disease and Rocky Mountain spotted fever are found throughout the west. To help prevent ticks latching on to you, tuck your pants legs into your socks, wear long sleeves, check yourself for ticks several times a day, and do a full-body check before you go to sleep at night. Consult a wilderness first-aid book for information on tick removal.

SUMMER ETHICS

In summer when the protective layer of snow is gone, we walk on exposed delicate subalpine and tundra ecosystems each time we step off the hut deck. Those waffle-stomper soles on your boots can destroy plant life at high elevations; please stay on designated trails, even if you're only going to the toilet, wood pile, or getting water.

Many people walk around a cabin in summer, and if everyone were to walk a different path, there would be fewer wildflowers returning each successive season. The negative impact of many heavy-footed humans on alpine tundra is one of the main arguments against summer hut use. If the areas around the huts are abused, huts will be forced to close in summer. Please, think before you step, stay on well-defined paths and tread lightly.

Avoid collapsing stream banks and lakeshores; don't stray form trails through meadows, stick to muddy trails and roads rather than create wider trails, and ford at designated stream crossings. It's important that hut users tread lightly to show land managers and others that the huts don't have to be detrimental to the environment.

Picking wildflowers for table arrangements may be illegal and is certainly unethical. Survival at high elevations where the growing season is short is difficult at best for plant life and any damage we cause may take decades to heal.

More people in the high country increases pressure on wildlife. Help protect wildlife by keeping noise levels to a minimum. Don't approach or spook animals. Dogs aren't allowed at most huts in the summer out of respect for wildlife. Just like the plant life at higher elevations, animals lead a harsh life. See Chapter 7, Natural Hazards for information on what to do if you encounter wildlife.

Designated wilderness areas neighbor many huts. In all wilderness areas, motorized and mechanized vehicles, including mountain bikes, are prohibited. Dogs must be on a leash.

When hiking, biking, climbing, or exploring, tread lightly and leave no trace. Cutting switchbacks causes erosion and trail damage. Motorized vehicles driven off of designated roads cause damage to tundra that may take a century or more to heal. We need to set an example for future generations as well as for our peers just being introduced to this fragile paradise.

Summer Gear

For hiking to the huts you need a backpack. An external-frame pack works fine, and is cooler than its more form-fitting winter internal-frame cousin. If you plan on climbing a few peaks, you may want to use an internal frame pack, since they fit closer to your body, and they will be less apt to cause you to lose your balance.

Your hiking boots will probably be a little lighter than your telemark boots, but hot spots and blisters still need to be treated the same. Rain gear and warm clothes should be part of your standard equipment. At the high elevation huts, evenings are very cool. You shouldn't need to bring your avalanche gear, but survival equipment is still important on a summer hut trip. You never know when something will happen that may prevent you from making it to the cabin. You might also want to bring bug repellent and gaiters for creek crossings and snowfields.

Mountain Bikes

Mountain biking is one of the fastest growing activities in North America, and biking to huts is becoming increasingly popular. Mountain bikers cover distance faster than a hiker, so cyclists may skip a hut or two in some systems. Others cycle into a hut, dump their gear, and spend two or three days riding around an area.

Mountain biking on public lands is relatively new, and courtesy will help win its lasting acceptance. Stay on designated trails, out of wilder-

Hiking and climbing are summer hut activities.
Photo by Scott Toepfer

ness areas, maintain safe speeds, and avoid shortcutting trails and skidding, which lead to erosion.

You have two ways to carry gear on your mountain bike. You can wear a backpack, which is clumsy, uncomfortable, and impractical, or use panniers, which attach to racks on your bike frame. If you decide on the latter, pack your panniers for a well-balanced load.

The most important thing to carry on a bike trip is a properly fitting helmet. Anyone who has crashed hard on their head with a helmet will tell you to wear one; many who have crashed hard on their heads without one can no longer tell you a thing.

Mountain biking at Big Creek Cabin, Colorado. Photo by Brian Litz

NATURAL HAZARDS

Using huts and yurts in summer can be a wonderfully rewarding experience, but it also poses certain dangers. Wildlife can be a problem. Lightning and thunderstorms are common. Weather changes rapidly and snow can fall any month of the year at higher elevations. If you plan on being away from the cabin for the day, carry warm clothes; you can get hypothermia in summer, too. See Chapter 7, *Natural Hazards* for more information.

COMPLAINT BOX

Just because you're a member of one of the hut associations or you spent a day there during the winter doesn't mean that you have carte blanche to wander into a cabin any time you want. One summer, while caretaking at NoName Hut, I was eating breakfast on the deck with three friends who had spent the night. Two gentleman walked onto the deck, right past us and into the cabin without so much as a how-do-you-do. They just walked right into my house! If someone were to do that in the city, they'd be shot. Their reasoning was that they had stayed at the hut last winter and so felt they could come anytime they wanted.

Please, always respect the privacy and rights of others when you visit the huts.

19

ACCESSIBILITY TO PEOPLE WITH DISABILITIES

Being the first blind man to experience the different dimensions here was a tremendous feeling. I have always said that sight is a distraction and blind stands for Beginning Life In a New Dimension.

—*T.N.*, from a hut logbook

A disability does not mean that someone cannot enjoy the hut experience. Several existing huts are accessible to people with disabilities, and more opportunities will be available as new huts are built under the requirements of the Americans with Disabilities Act (ADA).

If you have a disability or are thinking of bringing a friend with a disability to the huts, call the hut manager to find out about the hut and its access. ADA requires that huts accommodate people with a disabilities once they arrive, but it doesn't require a hard-surfaced, level-treaded trail with 2 percent grade so that a person with a mobility disability can get to the hut on his or her own. Nor does it require that motorized access be provided to the disabled person if it isn't permitted for other guests. One of the key aspects of ADA is that people with disabilities have the same opportunities as the other guests. Getting to the huts still requires backcountry travel, and a hut trip remains a backcountry experience for the guest with a disability.

We have a friend who brought his 80-year old grandmother-in-law and disabled brother-in-law to a hut by using a snowmobile for part of the journey and a ski-patrol sled to pull them the rest of the way to the hut. The family was able to enjoy an adventurous and memorable reunion in the backcountry.

Participants in a hut program with the Breckenridge Outdoor Education Center. Photo by Bob Winsett

Huts equipped for guests with disabilities have an entrance ramp instead of stairs, a larger restroom with turn-around space and grab bars, kitchen facilities with lower counters, sleeping accommodations on the main level, and fire alarms with strobe lights, in addition to other minor accommodations. In Colorado, Betty Bear Hut in the 10th Mountain system, and Francie's Cabin in the Summit Huts system are accessible to people with disabilities. The Breckenridge Outdoor Education Center is a non-profit organization that provides programs for people with disabilities and can take guests to Francie's Cabin.

QUOTABLES

At one time, people thought meeting the requirements of the Americans with Disabilities Act was ridiculous, questioning whether handicapped people would venture into the mountains in the summer, much less in the winter. Watching Joe Mead, a blind Forest Service employee from Washington, D.C., ski into Janet's Cabin virtually unassisted was an eye-opener for all of us. Joe had no problem staying on the trail by probing with his poles and following the voices of his companions. Once there, he even took telemark ski lessons from Gene Dayton of the Breckenridge Nordic Center. Last winter at Francie's Cabin, a spinal tumor disabled my right leg. Getting out was an interesting experience, but convinced me that even "disabled" travel will be possible for me. Next winter, if the control of these old legs doesn't improve much, I know it will still be possible to work my way in and out of some of these huts.
— Pete Wingle

20

OPERATIONS

Rome was not built in one day.
—*John Heywood (1497-1580)*

BUILDING A HUT

To build a hut requires vision, special planning, and governmental permission. Often the vision begins when an individual or family desires to memorialize a loved one by establishing a hut in his or her name. They work with a hut manager to name the cabin, sketch cabin designs, establish funding and endowment guidelines, and begin the permit-process with the land-management agency, such as the U.S. Forest Service. Funds to build the hut are raised through donations from family and friends, the community, and, occasionally, supportive foundations and other grant-making institutions.

Before the first clump of dirt is moved or construction begun, a hut manager must receive approval from the U.S. Forest Service, or the county government, if the hut is located on private land. Approval assumes that the hut system master plan has been approved by the Forest Service, and that a special-use permit has been granted. The environmental assessment process, which is required before a hut can be built, involves public input and evaluation by wildlife biologists, botanists, and archaeologists. Detailed plans must be developed for the hut itself, in which such considerations as capacity, access roads for construction, locations of outhouses and leach fields, operations, timing of construction, and other issues are addressed.

The construction of a hut is logistically difficult, expensive, and time consuming. Building at elevations over 11,000 feet, where all construction materials have to be carried in on rough, four-wheel-drive roads and where there's no building-supply center nearby requires special planning and expertise. The building season in Colorado, for example, is short, beginning in mid-July and ending by mid-October. Because of such limited building time, it can take two summers to build a hut. Construction crews may live and work on site to save time in transportation and wear and tear on their vehicles.

Francie's Cabin, in Colorado, under construction. Photo by Leigh Girvin Yule

FROM THE LOGBOOK

For all the many joys I've experienced at this very special place, I give thanks. I can feel the positive energy in this hut; it must be the result of a lot of thought, dedication, coalition building, memory, and pure hard labor. Thank you all. You have done beautiful work.

HUT OPERATIONS

It takes a small army to operate a hut system—reservations staff, operations managers, hut keepers, guides, and volunteers; all are equally important for a hut system to be successful.

The huts are usually supplied in autumn when motor-vehicle access is possible. As most hut access is by four-wheel-drive roads, pickup trucks and high-clearance vehicles are required, even for special needs like filling propane tanks and pumping out pit-toilet vaults. Hut managers truck in all the toilet paper, paper towels, aluminum foil, dish soap, and everything else needed to supply the hut for the winter. Firewood is also brought in, and numerous volunteers move and stack it.

The huts are given a thorough cleaning every season. Linens are hauled out and laundered, kitchens inventoried, damaged pots and pans replaced, chimneys swept, hardware fixed, and tools sharpened.

Summer and fall are the seasons for capital improvements and upgrades such as changes to the photovoltaic systems or replacing obsolete woodstoves.

Appalachian Mountain Club huts and Janet's Cabin in the Summit Huts system are especially challenging to maintain because the huts are inaccessible by road. They were built using materials brought in with pack animals or helicopters and continue to be supplied the same way.

At Janet's Cabin, all supplies must be organized and ready to fly to the hut on helicopter day. The propane tanks (which weigh about 800 pounds when full) are flown out empty to a waiting bulk truck, refilled, and flown back in to the hut. One or two cords of wood are loaded in a net and carried in a sling load under the helicopter. Janet's Cabin helicopter day is fast-paced, exhausting, and risky, but volunteers are rewarded with two nights in the hut for their efforts.

HUT VOLUNTEERS

Volunteers spend hundreds of hours building and maintaining trails, cleaning the huts, gathering and stacking firewood, and performing numerous forms of carpentry. They are usually paid for their help with credit for complimentary time in the hut.

During the season, a trained hut keeper will visit the cabin every one to two weeks to check on maintenance, clean the toilets, put out supplies, and police the system. Some hut keepers use snowmobiles to reach the huts and to bring in mid-winter supplies when they are needed. In the Summit Huts system, where snowmobiles aren't allowed, hut keepers ski to the cabins, and carry all supplies in sleds or on their backs. Some cabins have separate quarters for a the hutmaster, usually a simple bedroom that can be locked. Other cabins may have a complete apartment with cooking, sleeping, and living facilities.

Volunteers are always needed to help run hut systems. If you are interested in volunteering, contact the hut system manager for more information. A list of hut systems is included in Appendix B, Systems and Reservations Information.

Volunteers help get Janet's Cabin in Colorado ready for winter. Photo by Scott Toepfer

RULES AND POLICIES

Rules and policies vary depending on the hut and hut system. Check the hut instructions or ask the hut system manager or reservationists for specifics.

No Dogs

The no-dogs rule is almost universal at the huts and for good reason. The water supply at most of the hut and yurt systems is taken from melted snow near the structures, and dogs often relieve themselves in the snow. Dogs chase wild animals, bark, and fight, and some guests may be allergic to, afraid of, or simply dislike dogs. Many of the Colorado huts are governed by U.S. Forest Service regulations that prohibit dogs near the huts. Dog owners found violating the no-dog regulation are subject to fines and even time in jail.

The only exceptions to the no-dog rule are dogs trained for rescue and avalanche work when the dogs are there in connection with their official duties and service dogs for the disabled which are trained to urinate and defecate on command and are taken away from the hut to do so.

No Fireworks

No fireworks is a universal rule at all huts located on national forests. It is always illegal to set off fireworks in national forests because of the danger of wildfire, even on the Fourth of July or New Year's Eve.

No Firearms

Firearms are prohibited near the huts, most of which are closed during hunting season.

No Use without Reservation and Fee

With few exceptions, huts operate on a reservation and fee system. People who poach or crash the hut without making a reservation and paying their fee are trespassing and stealing services. For information on dealing with hut crashers, see Chapter 11, Problems at the Hut.

No Overcrowding

If you book an entire hut with an occupancy limit of twenty guests and you bring twenty-two you're considered to be poaching services. Overcrowding causes over-loading of toilets, extra wear and tear on the cabin, and drains supplies. Overcrowding at the hut also contributes to overcrowding in the backcountry.

Day Use

Some hut systems allow day visitors to eat lunch on the deck, use the restroom, and warm up, but only if overnight guests are already there and if the hut is open. In these systems, day users are allowed to use the hut only if the paying guests invite them to. Day visitors may be turned out. Dy visitors are not permitted to use the kitchen facilities or otherwise occupy the hut. Some hut systems do not allow day use at all because of the cabin's limited resources and out of respect for the privacy of paying guests.

Be sure to contact the hut system before planning any day visits to huts.

No Camping

Camping is generally prohibited near the huts as the space around the hut is considered to be a developed recreation area by the U.S. Forest Service which limits the kinds of use and number of people who can be there. Camping near the huts also causes over-crowding. Campers must stay at least one-fourth mile from the cabin.

Motorized Use

Some hut systems market to both the motorized and non-motorized user, but the governing philosophy for the majority of the huts is that the backcountry experience is one of self-sufficiency, which means you don't use motorized vehicles to carry you or your gear.

Many of the huts in Colorado's 10th Mountain and Summit systems have Forest Service regulations prohibiting motor vehicles near the cabins. This regulated non-motorized "envelope" varies from six to sixty acres or more, and preserves the quiet of the backcountry. Violators are subject to fines and possibly jail time.

Liability Waivers

Hut system managers require you to sign and return a liability release waiver. The huts may not be occupied by people who haven't done so.

Follow the Hut Instructions

Check and follow the hut instructions posted at each hut. These instructions include the rules applicable to that hut, as well as a listing of the user's responsibilities.

HUT SYSTEMS AND RESERVATIONS INFORMATION

UNITED STATES

California
Clair Tapaan Lodge
P.O. Box 36
Norden, CA 95724
916-426-3632

Colorado
Alfred Braun Memorial Hut System
P.O. Box 7937
Aspen, CO 81612
970-925-5775

This is Colorado's first hut system and is designed for the advanced backcountry skiers and mountaineers with strong legs and backs, map and compass skills, as well as avalanche awareness. These huts are not the place for beginning skiers. The trails are strenuous, the avalanche terrain is extensive and can be difficult to recognize, and some routes remain above treeline for long distances. Located in the Elk Range between Aspen and Crested Butte, the huts are much smaller and more rustic than their cousins in the 10th Mountain Division Hut Assoc-iation system. Due to their small size, there is not much room for your gear, and it will be more diffi-cult to find privacy, but the views and skiing here equal or exceed those found anywhere in Colorado. A mini-mum of four skiers is required to rent one of the huts. It is felt, and rightly so, that this is the safest number to have to travel to these huts. Once you gain com-petent mountaineering skills you will find the Alfred Braun system offers a lifetime of backcountry excitement.

Colorado Mountain Club
710 10th St. #200
Golden, CO 80401
303-279-3080

Colorado State Forest
Star Route, Box 91
Walden, CO 80480
970-723-8366

Continental Divide Hut System
228 N. F Street
Salida, CO 81201
1-800-288-0675

Diamond J Ranch
26604 Frying Pan Road
Meredith, CO 81642
970-927-3222

Elkton & Gothic Cabins
Crested Butte Nordic Center
512 Second Street
Crested Butte, CO 81224
970-349-6201

Hidden Treasure Yurt
P.O. Box 441
Edwards, CO 81632-0441
800-444-2813
970-926-4822

A lot of personal attention has been devoted to this yurt.

High Lonesome Hut
Box 145
Fraser, CO 80442
970-726-4099

A private hut whose owners will haul your gear by snowmobile if you request it.

Hinsdale Haute Route
P.O. Box 771
Lake City, CO 81224
970-944-2269

Lake Agnes Cabin
Colorado Division of Parks and
    Outdoor Recreation
P.O. Box 231
Littleton, CO 80160
800-678-2267

Mountain Creek Ranch
Box 134
Jefferson, CO 80456
303-789-1834

Never Summer Nordic Yurts
P.O. Box 1983
Fort. Collins, CO 80522
970-482-9411

Yurts are large-domed round canvas structures similar to the transportable animal-skin yurts used by Mongolian nomads. The Never Summer Nordic Yurts are in the Colorado State Forest west of Fort Collins. You will need a valid state-park pass, about $3.00, in order to use these yurts. These yurts sleep six. The set-up for the yurts is different than the huts. Living space is much more communal, and privacy will be a little harder to come by. Yurts warm quickly once a fire is going, but once the fire goes out, the yurts cool down much more rapidly than the insulated huts. This problem is easily remedied with a warm sleeping bag. If it gets really cold, someone may need to get up periodically to stoke the fire. Yurt trips are more like winter camping with a large well-appointed tent.

Southwest Nordic Center
P.O. Box 3212
Taos, NM 87571
505-758-4761

There are four yurts in the Cumbres Pass area on the Colorado-New Mexico border.

Saint Paul Lodge
P.O. Box 463
Silverton, CO 81433
970-387-5367

A quaint and unique lodge set in the spectacular San Juan Mountains. Available only with a guide and well worth it.

San Juan Hut System
P.O. Box 1663
Telluride, CO 81435
970-728-6935

The San Juan Hut System, like the Alfred Braun, requires more savvy and

skill to use than the Tenth and Summit systems. Most trails in the San Juan Systems are unmarked and considerable time can be spent above timberline where visibility can disappear rapidly during a snowstorm. Avalanche awareness, map and compass skills, and beefier gear are highly recommended for tours to huts in this system.

The four San Juan Huts and one yurt are located on the western end of the San Juan Mountains on the north side of the Sneffels Range in southern Colorado. Backcountry skiers will be hard pressed to find scenic beauty and quality skiing as fine as that outside the San Juan Hut System. Each of the small shelters sleeps up to ten people and is equipped with basic amenities.

Summit Huts Association
P.O. Box 2830
Breckenridge, CO 80424
Residence 970-925-5775
Office 970-453-8583

10th Division Mountain Hut
   Association
1280 Ute Avenue
Aspen, CO 81611
970-925-5775

These huts are well-appointed and comfortable, especially given their remote locations in Colorado's backcountry. Amenities include photovoltaic lighting, extensive libraries, and comfortable beds and seating areas. Some kitchens have both propane cooktops and wood-burning cookstoves, others have only propane burners. Toilets may be outdoor pit toilets or indoor composting toilets.

The designated trails to the TMDHA and SHA huts are designed to avoid avalanche terrain as much as possible. Most of these huts have more than one route and trailhead, some easier, some harder.

Tennessee Mountain Cabin
Eldora Nordic Center
P.O. Box 430
Nederland, CO 80466
303-440-8700

Eastern United States

Adirondack Mountain Club
91 Main Street
Lake Placid, NY 12946
518-899-2725

Appalachian Mountain Club
5 Joy Street
Boston, MA 02108
Residence 603-466-2727
Office 617-523-0636

Dartmouth Outing Club
Box 9
Hanover, NH 03755
603-646-2428

You must be a member or a guest of a member to reserve one of their nine cabins.

Mountain Recreation, Inc.
P.O. Box 1076
Conway, NH 03818
603-447-1786

Hawaii

Haleakala National Park
Superintendant
Box 369
Makawao, Maui, HI 96768

This system has three cabins which are mainly summer-use cabins: Holua Cabin, Kapalaoa Cabin, Paliku Cabin

Idaho:

Most of the cabins and lookouts in the Clearwater and Idaho Panhandle National Forests are rustic and you need to bring kitchen supplies. Call the National Forest Office listed for information on specific huts.

Clearwater National Forest
12730 Highway 12
Orofino, ID 83544
208-476-4541

Idaho Panhandle National Forest
3815 Schreiber Way
Coeur d'Alene, ID 83814-8363
208-765-7223

Sun Valley Trekking
P.O. Box 2200
Sun Valley, ID 83353
208-622-5371

Five huts honored as one of North America's top hut systems by *Snow Country Magazine.*

Timberland Trails of Idaho, Inc
c/o Mountain Recreation, Inc.
P.O. Box 1076
Conway, NH 03818
603-447-1786

This is part of the Mountain Recreation, Inc. national hut and trail system on private land. It will feature four-season base lodges and a trail system for all ability levels through forests and to alpine summits. It's part of the International Youth Hostel System. Huts are anticipated to be ready for use in 1997.

Wilderness River Outfitters
P.O. Box 871
Salmon, ID 83467
800-252-6581

Minnesota

Boundary Country Trekking
590 Gunflint Trail
Grand Marais, MN 53604
800-322-8327

Montana

Huts and cabins in Montana are more primitive than most hut systems. You may need to provide your own firewood, cookstoves, pots, pans, and other kitchen necessities. Many of the cabins require long tours, some twenty miles or longer, making snowmobile support very handy. Call the National Forest Office listed for information on specific huts.

Northern Region Headquarters
USDA Forest Service
P.O. Box 7669
Missoula, MT 59807
406-329-3511

Beaverhead National Forest
420 Barrett Street
Dillon, MT 59725-3572
406-683-3900

Bitterroot National Forest
1801 N. First Street
HW 93 N
Hamilton, MT 59840
406-363-7161

Custer National Forest
2602 First Avenue North
P.O. Box 2556
Billings, MT 59103
406-657-6361

Deerlodge National
Forest Federal Building
400 N. Main, P.O. Box 400
Butte, MT 59703
406-496-3400

Flathead National Forest
1935 Third Avenue East
Kalispell, MT 59901
406-755-5401

Gallatin National Forest
Federal Building
10 East Babcock Avenue
P.O. Box 130,
Bozeman, MT 59771
406-587-6920

Helena National Forest
2880 Skyway Drive
Helena, MT 59601
406-449-5201

Kootenai National Forest
506 U.S. Highway 2 West
Libby, MT 59923
406-293-6211

Lewis and Clark National Forest
1101 15th Street N.
P.O. Box 869
Great Falls, MT 59801
406-791-7700

Lolo National Forest
Building 24, Fort Missoula
Missoula, MT 59801
406-329-3750

Oregon
Silcox Hut
503-297-2165

Wing Ridge Ski Tours
P.O. Box 714
Joseph, OR 97846
800-646-905ʊ

Utah
La Sal Huts
452 N. Main
Moab, Utah 84532
801-259-8946

Powder Ridge Backcountry Yurts
545 West, 3200 South
Nibley, UT 84321
801-752-7853

Tag-A-Long Expeditions
800-453-3292

Incredible scenery of the red rock
desert country of Utah.

Washington
Rendezvous Outfitters
P.O. Box 728
Winthrop, WA 98862
509-996-3299

Scottish Lakes
c/o High Country Adventures
P.O. Box 2023
Snoquamish, WA 98291-2023
206-844-2000

CANADA
Alpine Club of Canada Huts
403-678-3200

Banff National Park Huts
403-762-4256

BC Forest Service Huts
604-342-4200

Blanket Glacier Chalet*
Nordic Ski Institute
Box 1050
Canmore, Alberta TOL OMO
403-678-4102

Dave Henry Lodge*
Headwaters Outfitting Ltd.
Box 818
Valemount, BC VOE 2ZO
604-566-4718

Durrand Glacier Chalet*
Selkirk Mountain Experience Ltd.
P.O. Box 2998
Revelstoke, BC VOE 2SO
604-837-2381
selkirk@junction.net

Esplanade Range Chalets*
Golden Alpine Holidays
Box 1050
Golden, BC VOA 1HO
604-344-7273

Island Lake Mountain Tours[†]
Cedar Valley Road
Fernie, BC VOB 1M1
604-423-3700

Mistaya Lodge*
Box 809
Golden, BC VOA 1HO
604-344-6689

Misty Mountain Hut[∫]
Box 1073
Kaslo, BC VOG 1MO
604-353-7557

Monashee Chalet[§]
Interior Alpine Recreation
P.O. Box 1528
Kamloops, BC V2C 6L8
604-522-1239

North Rockies Ski Tours*
1960 Garden Drive
Prince George, BC V2M 2V8
604-564-7814

Ptarmigan Tours*
Box 11
Kimberley, BC V1A 2Y5
604-422-3566

Purcell Lodge*
ABC Wilderness Adventures
P.O. Box 1829
Golden, BC VOA 1HO
604-344-2639

Selkirk Lodge*
Box 1409
Golden, BC VOA 1HO
604-344-5016

Sorcerer Lake Lodge*
Box 175
Golden, BC VOA 1HO
604-344-2326

Swift Creek Cabins*
Headwaters Outfitting Ltd
Box 818
Valemount, BC VOE 2ZO
604-566-4718

Valhalla Lodge*
Box 1167
Kaslo, BC VOG 1MO
604-353-7179

Wells Gray Park Backcountry Chalets*
Box 188
Clearwater, BC VOE 1NO
604-587-6444

*   accessible by helicopter only
**   accessible by helicopter, skis, or
       snocat
∫   accessible by helicopter or skis
†   accessible by snocat only
§   accessible by snocat or skis

AVALANCHE INFORMATION

UNITED STATES

Avalanche Hotline
Cyberspace Snow & Avalanche Center http://www.cfac.org

California
Central-Eastern Sierra (Mammoth Lakes) 619-934-6611
Lake Tahoe/Donner Summit (Truckee) 916-587-2158

Colorado
Aspen 970-920-1664
Colorado Springs 719-520-0020
Denver 303-275-5360
Durango 970-247-8187
Fort Collins 970-482-0457
Summit County 970-668-0600
Vail 970-827-5687

Idaho
Smokey, Sawtooth, and Pioneer Mountains (Ketchum) 208-788-1200, x8027

Montana
Northwest Montana Rockies (Kalispell) 406-758-5368
South Central Mountains (Bozeman) 406-587-6981
Southern Mountains (Cooke City) 406-838-2259
Southern Mountains (West Yellowstone) 406-646-7912
West Central Mountains (Missoula) 406-549-4488

Oregon
S. Washington Cascades and Mt. Hood (Portland) 503-326-2400

Utah
La Sal Mountains (Moab) 801-259-7669
North Wasatch (Logan) 801-797-4146
Mt. Ogden south to Tri-Canyons 801-621-2362
Park City Area (East Of Tri-Canyon) 801-649-2250
Sundance/Mt. Timpanogos Area (Provo) 801-374-9770
Tri-Canyon Area (Salt Lake City) 801-364-1581

Washington
Washington Cascades and Olympics (Seattle) 206-526-6677

Wyoming
Teton, Wyoming and Wind River Range 307-733-2664

CANADA

Banff National Park 403-762-1460
Canadian Rockies 403-243-7253, x7669
Canada (Vancouver area) 604-290-9333
E-mail canav@mindlink.bc.ca

EQUIPMENT MANUFACTURERS

Hardware Manufacturers

Adventures To The Edge
P.O. Box 91
Crested Butte, CO 81224
970-349-5219
800-349-5219

Rescue sleds and outdoor oriented courses

Alpine Trekker
4949 North Broadway
Boulder, CO 80304
800-670-8735
303-417-1345

Alpine binding insert converters for Randonée

Life-Link International, Inc
P.O. Box 2913
Jackson, WY 83001
307-733-2266

Avalanche related equipment

Mountain Smith
18301 West Colfax Avenue
Golden, CO 80401
303-279-5930

Packs and sleds

Mountain Safety Research
P.O. Box 24547
Seattle, WA 98124
800-877-9677

Stoves, water filters

Ramer Products, Ltd.
1803 South Foothills Highway
Boulder, CO 80303-7366
303-499-4466
Alpine touring equipment

Sports Rent
560 S. Holly Street
Denver, CO 80222
303-320-0222

Avalanche equipment and beacon rental

Tua Ski
1945 33rd Street
Boulder, CO 80301
303-417-0301

Voilé
2636 South 2700 West
Salt Lake City, UT 84119
801-973-8622

Avalanche rescue equipment and bindings

Wasatch Touring
702 East 100 South
Salt Lake City, UT 84101
801-359-9361

Software Manufacturers

Marmot Mountain Ltd.
2321 Circadian Way
Santa Rosa, CA 95407
707-544-5490

North Face
2013 Farallon Drive
San Leandro, CA 94577
800-362-4963

Patagonia
P.O. Box 150
Ventura, CA 93002
805-643-8616

EQUIPMENT LISTS

This list is only a guideline. You may have other things which are essential to you that you'll want to bring. Other lists are found throughout the book. As you spend more time in the backcountry you will discover certain things to add to your list. Write them down in your notepad. A really nice-to-bring item is a clean set of clothes and comfortable pair of shoes to leave in your car at the trailhead; it makes the trip home much more pleasant.

Winter Gear
Sleeping bag
Long underwear (tops and bottoms)
Fleece pants (for wearing around the hut)
Medium weight shirt
Heavy pile or wool sweater
Socks
Down vest or sweater
Hut slippers
Mountain parka or wind and snow shell (with hood)
Wind and snow shell pants
Two pairs of gloves (or mittens), both light- and heavyweight
Ski hat
Neck gaiter or scarf
Gaiters
Sunglasses and goggles
Baseball cap or sun hat

Equipment
Skis, boots and poles, or snowshoes
Climbing skins and/or wax
Backpack (medium to large capacity, 3,000 to 6,000 cubic inches)
Stuff sacks
Day pack or fanny pack
Headlamp or flashlight
Spare batteries
Sunscreen and lip balm
Maps and guidebooks

Altimeter
Compass
Snow-pit kit for avalanche analysis
Shovel
Avalanche transceiver (beacon)
Avalanche probes or probe ski-poles
Pad
Water bottles
First aid kit
Toilet paper
Ski repair kit

Ski Repair Kit
Duct tape
Spare ski tip
Steel wool
Spare ski pole basket
Pocketknife or Leatherman

Wire
Parachute cord
Screws
Spare binding parts
Sewing kit

Survival Kit
Mirror
Lighter and matches
drinks
Pocketknife
Heat packs
Space Blanket
Long-burning candles
Stove and pot

Note pad and pencil
High-energy snacks and

Stove repair kit
Webbing
Safety pins
Bivouac sack or tarp

Bike Repair Kit
Tire levers (to change flat tires)
Patch kit
Spare tube(s)
Assorted wrenches (Allen wrenches
    and open-ended wrenches)
Small Phillips head and standard screwdrivers

Chain oil and chain
Duct tape
Tire pump
Spare parts
Electricians tape

Special Summer Gear
Bug repellent
Rain gear
Lightweight wool sweater

Water filter
Hiking boots
Gaiters

BIBLIOGRAPHY

Armstrong, Betsy R., Knox Williams, and Chuck Tolton, *Avalanche Awareness: A Question of Balance*, video. Denver, CO: 1988.

Armstrong, Betsy R. and Knox Williams, *The Avalanche Book*. Golden, CO: Fulcrum Publishing, 1992.

Auerbach, Paul S., editor, *Wilderness Medicine: Management of Wilderness and Environmental Emergencies*, 3rd Edition. St. Louis, MO: Mosby Press.

Axcell, Claudia, Diana Cooke, and Vicki Kinmont, *Simple Foods for the Pack*. San Francisco, CA: Sierra Club Books, 1986.

Cliff, Peter, *Ski Mountaineering*. Seattle, WA: Pacific Search Press, 1987.

Clifford, Harlan C., "Fritz Benedict: Founder of the 10th Mountain Division Hut Association," *Adventure West*, Winter/Spring 1994.

Coolidge, W.A.B., *The Alps in Nature and History*. New York, NY: E.P. Dutton Co., 1908.

Dawson, Lou, editor, *10th Mountain Trail* and *10th Mountain Division Hut Association*, newsletters, Vol. 1 No. 1 through Vol. 9, No. 1, January 1988-April 1996.

Dawson, Lou, W. II, *Colorado 10th Mountain Trails*. Aspen, CO: WHO Press, 1989.

Hackett, Peter, *Mountain Sickness: Prevention, Recognition and Treatment*. New York, NY: AAC Press, 1980.

Herzog, Maurice, *Annapurna*. Salem, NY: The Adventure Library, 1995.

Johnson, Tom, and Tim Miller, *The Sauna Book*. New York, NY: Harper and Row Publishers, Inc., 1977.

Kjellstrom, Bjorn, *Be Expert with Map and Compass: The Orienteering Handbook*. New York, NY: Charles Scribner & Sons, 1976.

Litz, Brian, *Colorado Hut to Hut*. Englewood, CO: Westcliffe Publishers, 1992.

Lunn, Arnold, *A History of Ski-ing*. London: Oxford University Press, 1927.

McClung, David, and Peter Schaerer, *The Avalanche Handbook*. Seattle, WA: The Mountaineers, 1993.

McHugh, Gretchen, *The Hungry Hiker's Book of Good Cooking*. New York, NY: Alfred A. Knopf, Inc., 1982.

Meyer, Kathleen, *How to Shit in the Woods*. Berkeley, CA: Ten Speed Press, 1989.

Mitchell, Dick, *Mountaineering First Aid: A Guide to Accident Response and First Aid Care*, 2nd edition. Seattle, WA: The Mountaineers, 1975.

Parker, Paul, *Free-Heel Skiing: Telemark and Parallel Techniques for All Conditions.* Seattle, WA: The Mountaineers, 1995.

Peters, Ed, editor, *Mountaineering: Freedom of the Hills,* 4th edition. Seattle, WA: The Mountaineers, 1982.

Randall, Glenn, The *Outward Bound Map and Compass Book.* New York, NY: Lyons & Burford, Publishers, 1989.

Reifsnyder, William E., *High Huts of the White Mountains,* 2nd Edition. Boston, MA: Appalachian Mountain Club Books, 1993.

Roberts, Eric, *High Level Route.* Reading England: West Col Productions, 1973.

Schimelpfenig, Tod and Linda Lindsey, *NOLS Wilderness First Aid,* 2nd edition. Lander, WY: National Outdoor Leadership School and Stackpole Books, 1992.

Scott, Chic, *Summits and Icefields.* Calgary, Alberta: Rocky Mountain Books, 1994.

Setnicke, Tim, *Wilderness Search and Rescue.* Boston, MA: Appalachian Mountain Club, 1980.

Stewart, Chris, and Mike Torrey, editors, *Century of Hospitality in High Places: The Appalachian Mountain Club Hut System, 1888-1988.* Boston, MA: The Appalachian Mountain Club, 1988.

Tolkien, J.R.R., *The Fellowship Of The Ring.* New York, NY: Ballantine Books, Inc., 1972.

Wilkerson, James A., *Medicine for Mountaineering,* 2nd edition. Seattle, WA: The Mountaineers, 1975.

INDEX

ABOUT THE AUTHORS AND CONTRIBUTORS

Authors Leigh Girvin Yule and Scott Toepfer. Photo taken by Scott Toepfer (with the aid of a timed shutter release).

Scott Toepfer

Scott works winters as a mountain weather and avalanche forecaster for the Colorado Avalanche Information Center. During the summer he has his own construction business. He also is a board member of Summits Huts Association, as well as a winter caretaker at Janet's and Francie's Cabins. Most of his spare time is spent bike riding, climbing, camping, or skiing.

Leigh Girvin Yule

Leigh is executive director of Summit Huts Association and has been involved with the organization in various capacities since 1987. Leigh fell in love with cross-country skiing shortly after she moved to Colorado with her family in 1972. She now enjoys all free-heel-skiing disciplines, as well as bicycling, hiking, and gardening. Leigh lives with her husband and two cats in Breckenridge, Colorado.

Dale Atkins

Dale is the U.S. representative to the International Commission on Alpine Rescue. He has been an avalanche forecaster at the Colorado Avalanche Information Center since 1987, with the Alpine Rescue Team in Evergreen, Colorado since 1974, and has served as a professional ski patroller at Loveland Ski Area since 1983.

John Cooley

John has been involved in the outdoor industry for more than twenty-five years as a professional guide, educator, commissioned salesman, and entrepreneur. He is the vice president of marketing, and an officer and employee-owner of Marmot Mountain Ltd. in California. An attorney by education and a mountaineer by avocation, John has climbed two 8,000 meter peaks, Makalu in Nepal and Xixabangma in Tibet as a member of the first American ascent team. He has climbing and skiing experience throughout North America, Asia and Europe, including eight randonée routes.

Paul Parker

Paul has been telemark skiing for twenty-five years. Formerly a member of the Professional Ski Instructors of America's Nordic Demonstration Team, he is a certified ski instructor in both Nordic and Alpine disciplines. Involved for many years in the sport's rapidly changing technologies, including boot and ski design, he currently works as a product development consultant for Tua and Asolo, and manages ski products for Patagonia. He lives in Breckenridge, Colorado.

Chris Pizzo, M.D.

Chris is a Denver-based pathologist with a background in high-altitude physiology research. He has lived in Colorado for more than twenty years and has extensive international mountaineering experience. As a member of a medical research expedition in 1981, he became the first person to collect human physiologic data at the summit of Mt. Everest. Chris is a member of the Honorary Board of Directors of Summit Huts Association.

John G. Warner, D.D.S.

John is a founder of Summit Huts Association and has been its Board President since 1987. He has enjoyed hut skiing for over thirteen years in Colorado, Canada, and Europe. John lives with his wife and two young daughters in Breckenridge, Colorado, where he has practiced general dentistry since 1980. In his spare time, John enjoys biking, all types of skiing, running, photography, tennis, and travel.

Pete Wingle

Pete is a retired U.S. Forest Service regional staff director and forest supervisor who has been a board member of 10th Mountain Division Hut Association since 1983 and Summit Huts Association since 1991. Pete is also a member of the Colorado Ski Hall of Fame. His backcountry skiing interests have taken him to Canada, Uzbekistan, the Swiss and French Alps, and across the U.S.A.